Dedicated to

Dedicated to my Father, my first Guru who had been instrumental in teaching and guidance throughout my entire life

पिता स्वर्गः पिता धर्मः पिता परमकं तपः ।
पितरि प्रीतिमापन्ने सर्वाः प्रीयन्ति देवताः ॥

Transliteration:

pitā svargaḥ pitā dharmaḥ pitā paramakaṃ tapaḥ ।
pitari prītimāpanne sarvāḥ prīyanti devatāḥ ॥

Hindi translation:

मेरे पिता मेरे स्वर्ग हैं, मेरे पिता मेरे धर्म हैं, वे मेरे जीवन की परम तपस्या हैं।
जब वे खुश होते हैं, तब सभी देवता खुश होते हैं !

English translation:

My Father is my heaven, my father is my dharma, he is the ultimate penance of my life. If he is happy,
all deities are pleased.

Source: Mahabharata Shanti Parva 258.20

DISCLAIMER

This book is intended to provide general information and guidance on how to do business in India. It is not a substitute for professional advice or services. The author and the publisher do not guarantee the accuracy, completeness, or suitability of the information and opinions expressed in this book for any specific purpose or situation. The reader is advised to consult with a qualified professional before taking any action based on the contents of this book.

The author and the publisher are not responsible for any errors or omissions in this book or for any consequences arising from the use of this book. The author and the publisher do not endorse or recommend any products, services, websites, or organizations mentioned in this book. The views and opinions expressed in this book are solely those of the author and do not necessarily reflect those of the publisher or any other person or entity.

The author and the publisher have taken all reasonable care to ensure that the information and opinions in this book are current and accurate as of the date of publication. However, the business environment in India is constantly changing and evolving. Therefore, the reader is advised to verify the latest developments and updates before relying on any information or opinion in this book.

This book is protected by copyright laws. No part of this book may be reproduced, distributed, transmitted, or stored in any form or by any means without the prior written permission of the author and the publisher.

You can use the information in this book for academic purposes if you acknowledge the source and give proper credit to the author and the publisher. You should also follow academic writing and citation's ethical and legal norms. You should not copy, plagiarize, or misrepresent any information or opinion in this book. You

2

should also respect the author's and the publisher's intellectual property rights.

FOREWORDS

How to Do Business in India: A Practical Guide for Entrepreneurs and Intrapreneurs

India is a land of opportunities and challenges for anyone who wants to start or grow a business. With a population of over 1.3 billion, a diverse and dynamic market, a vibrant and innovative ecosystem, and a supportive and reform-oriented government, India offers immense potential for entrepreneurs and intrapreneurs alike.

But doing business in India is not easy. It requires a deep understanding of the cultural, social, economic, legal, and political aspects of the country. It also requires a lot of patience, perseverance, and passion to overcome the various hurdles and risks that come along the way. Many a times my student participants expressed a dire need for such a handbook as a ready reckoner for themselves.

That is why I authored this book. To share with you my insights and experiences of doing business in India for over two decades. To help you navigate the complexities and nuances of the Indian market. To inspire you to pursue your dreams and aspirations with confidence and courage.

This book is for you if:
- You are an entrepreneur who wants to start or scale up your own business in India.
- You are an intrapreneur who wants to innovate or expand your existing business in India.
- You are a student or a professional who wants to learn more about the opportunities and challenges of doing business in India.
- You are a NRI who wants to return to India with an idea to start-up a business.
- A multinational company who wants to set up his establishment in India.

4

- You are tired of your job and want to get into your entrepreneurial journey.

In this book, you will learn:

- How to identify and validate your business idea or opportunity in India.
- How to create and execute your business plan or strategy in India.
- How to raise funds and manage your finances in India.
- How to build and lead your team and culture in India.
- How to market and sell your products or services in India.
- How to deal with customers, partners, competitors, regulators, and stakeholders in India.
- How to overcome the common pitfalls and problems of doing business in India.
- How to leverage the best practices and success stories of other entrepreneurs and intrapreneurs in India.

This book is not a theoretical or academic treatise. It is a practical and actionable guide that draws from my own journey as a teacher, trainer and mentor for several entrepreneurs and intrapreneurs in India. It also features a few case studies of some of the most successful and influential business leaders in emerging India.

My father used to tell me to start-up a business when I just passed out of engineering college. However, I decided to gain experience and choose wage employment. I have received several chances to work as an intrapreneur for several multinational organizations because my job functions were Sales, Business Development and other aspects of Marketing.

I have learned a lot from my mentors, peers, customers, and competitors especially working with National Institute for MSME (**ni-msme**). The website is www.nimsme.org This institute is known as the mother of entrepreneurship in India established in the 1960, where the myth is broken that entrepreneurs are not born, they can be also raised by training and mentoring. I have also made a lot of mistakes and faced several failures as an individual. But I never gave up on my dreams. Ultimately experiences are all the accumulation of learnings out of failures only.

I want to share with you my experiences and my lessons. I want to help you achieve your goals and ambitions. I want to show you how to do business in India.

Are you ready?
Let us begin.

Dr. Dibyendu Choudhury

P.S: For any comments or clarifications the author can be reached anytime through his website www.dibyenduchoudhury.com

Contents

INTRODUCTION

Aspiring entrepreneurs can capitalize on India's massive population and quickly expanding economy by taking use of the country's many available chances. However, in order to successfully navigate the intricate commercial landscape of India, one must have an in-depth knowledge of the myriad of elements that influence the market. For entrepreneurs to be able to make educated choices and get their businesses off the ground, they need access to information about key economic indicators, cultural aspects, the legal and regulatory environment, market research, technology and innovation, sustainability and social responsibility, and sector-specific insights.

The enormous consumer market that comprises India, which has a population of more than 1.3 billion people, offers enormous chances for business owners to capitalize on. The expanding middle class and rising purchasing power allow business owners to target a ready-made customer base. India's competent workforce, particularly in the technology sector, can be capitalized to establish a formidable team for technology startups, consulting firms, manufacturing organizations, or social enterprises. This is particularly true in India's case because of the country's large and growing middle class. Businesses have an advantage over their competitors, thanks to the relatively low cost of labour in India when compared to the cost of labour in other nations and the supportive Government ecosystem. That is how India has emerged as the fifth-largest economy in the world and will emerge as the third-largest economy within a few years.

It is also important to highlight the supporting ecosystem that India has created for start-up businesses. Initiatives such as the "Make in India" campaign and the "Startup India" programme attempt to simplify the regulatory processes, offer financial support and produce an atmosphere that is favourable to the success of start-up businesses. However, business owners have a responsibility to be aware of the complicated regulatory environment, which can be intimidating for those who are just starting out. In addition, there may be deficiencies in the infrastructure, particularly in areas such as transportation and logistics, which may interfere with the normal operation of enterprises. If entrepreneurs have a good awareness of the Indian business ecosystem, they will be able to efficiently handle hurdles and capitalize on the tremendous opportunities that are accessible. Beginning a business in India has enormous prospects in a wide variety of fields, but prospective business owners need to be aware of the country's complicated regulatory environment and its limited infrastructure resources.

In conclusion, in order for entrepreneurs to achieve success in their chosen industry, it is essential for them to be able to recognize emerging technological trends and successfully navigate the challenging landscape of beginning a business in India. This section offers entrepreneurs in India who are interested in growing and scaling their tech startups useful information and resources to help them do it. The ecosystem for software startups in India is expanding at a rapid rate, offering enormous possibilities for business owners who can successfully navigate the environment. To be successful, entrepreneurs need to have an understanding of the vast and diverse market, adapt their product or service to cater to regional preferences, cultural diversity, and the digital divide between urban and rural areas, build a dedicated team, secure funding, establish strategic partnerships, and embrace sustainability and social impact. Only then they can hope to achieve economic and social success.

Entrepreneurs who are interested in starting a business would find India to be an attractive location due to the country's constantly expanding population and economy. However, as a result of this growth, business owners have an increasingly urgent requirement to modify their goods and services so that they may better address the specific requirements of the Indian market. Increasing one's talent pool can be helped by making investments in productive workplace culture, attractive salary packages, and chances for skill development. The formation of strategic alliances and collaborations with established enterprises, incubators, accelerators, and government organizations can give significant support and resources that can facilitate growth. To summarize, growing and scaling a software startup in India is a fascinating journey that is full of opportunities and challenges. Entrepreneurs should position themselves for success in this dynamic ecosystem by gaining a grasp of the Indian market, forming an ardent team, acquiring capital, establishing strategic relationships, and embracing sustainability in their business practices.

I am sure this one book might not capture all the requirements of all the entrepreneurs from different segments. Because of the complexities of the entire eco-system one size may not fit all, however with this book the idea about the Indian entrepreneurial journey can be started.

CHAPTER-1

INTRODUCTION TO STARTING A BUSINESS IN INDIA

*it's time to celebrate
your moment
& charge your body*

@dibyenduchoudhury

CHAPTER 1: INTRODUCTION TO STARTING A BUSINESS IN INDIA

Understanding the Indian Business Landscape

India, with its vast population and rapidly growing economy, presents a plethora of opportunities for aspiring entrepreneurs. However, to navigate the complex and diverse Indian business landscape, it is essential to have a comprehensive understanding of the numerous factors that shape the market. This subchapter aims to provide aspiring entrepreneurs with valuable insights into the Indian business landscape, enabling them to make informed decisions and successfully start their ventures.

1. **Economic Overview:** India, as one of the fastest-growing economies in the world, offers immense potential for business growth. Understanding key economic indicators, such as GDP growth, inflation rates, and government policies, is crucial for entrepreneurs to identify viable business opportunities and mitigate risks.

2. **Cultural Factors:** India's rich cultural heritage significantly influences its business environment. Entrepreneurs must comprehend the nuances of Indian culture, including social hierarchies, communication styles, and business etiquette. These insights will help establish strong relationships with clients, suppliers, and employees, fostering successful business operations.

3. **Legal and Regulatory Environment:** Navigating India's legal and regulatory framework can be challenging for entrepreneurs. Familiarity with company registration processes, tax laws, intellectual property rights, and labor

regulations is essential. Engaging legal counsel and seeking professional advice will ensure compliance and safeguard the business's interests.

4. **Market Research:** Conducting comprehensive market research is crucial to identify target customers, analyze competitors, and understand consumer behavior. Entrepreneurs should gather data on market size, consumer preferences and trends specific to their niche to develop effective business strategies and gain a competitive edge.

5. **Technology and Innovation:** India's tech landscape is thriving, offering immense opportunities for tech startups. Entrepreneurs must stay updated on emerging technologies, government initiatives, and digital infrastructure to leverage these advancements. Collaborating with local tech communities and fostering innovation will enhance the chances of success in the tech startup ecosystem.

6. **Sustainability and Social Responsibility:** In recent years, sustainability and social responsibility have gained significant traction in India. Aspiring entrepreneurs should consider integrating sustainable practices into their business models, addressing environmental concerns, and contributing to social welfare. This approach not only aligns with changing consumer preferences but also enhances the brand's reputation and attracts conscious consumers.

7. **Sector-Specific Insights:** For entrepreneurs targeting specific sectors like consulting, manufacturing, or social enterprises, understanding industry-specific dynamics is crucial. Identifying industry trends, regulatory requirements, and supply chain considerations will help entrepreneurs develop focused business plans and establish a strong foothold in their chosen niche.

By gaining a thorough understanding of the Indian business landscape, aspiring entrepreneurs can navigate challenges effectively and capitalize on the vast opportunities available. This subchapter serves as a valuable resource, helping entrepreneurs in various niches, including starting a tech startup, sustainable business, consulting, manufacturing, and social enterprise, embark on their entrepreneurial journey with confidence and success.

Benefits and Challenges of Starting a Business in India:

Benefits and Challenges of Starting a Business in India

Aspiring Entrepreneurs, whether their interests lie in starting a tech startup, a sustainable business, a consulting firm, a manufacturing business, or a social enterprise, will find India to be a promising destination. With its booming economy, vast consumer base, and supportive ecosystem, India offers numerous advantages for those looking to turn their ideas into reality. However, like any entrepreneurial journey, there are also challenges to be navigated. In this subchapter, we will explore the benefits and challenges of starting a business in India to help you make informed decisions and set realistic expectations.

One of the key advantages of starting a business in India is the massive consumer market. With a population of over 1.3 billion people, India presents immense opportunities for entrepreneurs to tap into. Whether you are offering tech solutions, sustainable products, consulting services, or manufacturing goods, the sheer size of the Indian market can fuel your growth and revenue potential. Additionally, India's growing middle class and increasing purchasing power provide a ready customer base for entrepreneurs to target.

Another benefit of starting a business in India is the availability of a skilled workforce. India boasts a large pool of talented and educated professionals, especially in the technology sector. This talent pool can be leveraged to build a dedicated team for your tech startup, consulting firm, or manufacturing business. Moreover, the cost of labor in India is relatively lower compared to other countries, providing a competitive advantage for businesses.

India's supportive ecosystem for startups is also worth noting. The government has launched several initiatives and programs to foster entrepreneurship, such as the "Make in India" campaign and the "Startup India" initiative. These initiatives aim to ease regulatory processes, provide funding support, and create a conducive environment for startups to thrive. Aspiring entrepreneurs can take advantage of these resources to kickstart their ventures.

Despite the numerous benefits, there are challenges that entrepreneurs need to be aware of. One such challenge is the complex regulatory environment. India has a plethora of laws and regulations that businesses must adhere to, which can be overwhelming for newcomers. Navigating through the bureaucratic processes and ensuring compliance with legal requirements can be time-consuming and require professional assistance.

Infrastructure, particularly in areas like transportation and logistics, is another challenge entrepreneurs may face. While India has made considerable progress in improving its infrastructure, there are still gaps that can impact the smooth functioning of businesses. Entrepreneurs need to carefully consider these challenges and plan accordingly to mitigate their impact on operations.

In conclusion, starting a business in India offers immense opportunities across various niches. The benefits of a large consumer market, skilled workforce, and supportive ecosystem make India an attractive destination for aspiring entrepreneurs. However, it is crucial to be aware of the challenges, including complex regulations and infrastructure limitations. By understanding and addressing these challenges, entrepreneurs can navigate the Indian business landscape more effectively and increase their chances of success.

Legal and Regulatory Framework in India

Starting a business in India requires a thorough understanding of the legal and regulatory framework that governs business operations in the country. This subchapter aims to provide aspiring entrepreneurs with an overview of the key legal and regulatory aspects to consider when starting a business in India.

India has a robust legal system that encompasses various laws and regulations governing various aspects of business operations. The primary legislation that governs business entities in India is the Companies Act, which defines the structure and functioning of diverse types of companies. Entrepreneurs must familiarize themselves with the requirements for registering with a company, such as obtaining a Director Identification Number (DIN) and Digital Signature Certificate (DSC), and the process of obtaining necessary approvals and licenses.

Additionally, entrepreneurs planning to start a tech startup, or a manufacturing business should be aware of intellectual property rights (IPR) laws in India. Protecting inventions, trademarks, and copyrights is crucial to safeguarding one's business interests. Understanding the process of obtaining patents, trademarks, and copyrights, and the importance of maintaining confidentiality and non-disclosure agreements is essential for entrepreneurs operating in these niches.

For those interested in starting a sustainable business or social enterprise, it is important to familiarize themselves with the environmental laws and regulations in India. Compliance with environmental norms is critical to ensure sustainable operations and avoid penalties or legal challenges. Entrepreneurs must understand the process of obtaining necessary environmental clearances and permits, as well as the obligations and reporting requirements related to waste management, pollution control, and conservation.

Consulting businesses, on the other hand, need to be aware of regulations related to professional services, including licensing requirements and codes of conduct. Understanding the legal framework governing professional services and maintaining compliance with ethical standards is vital for success in this niche.

Overall, starting a business in India requires a comprehensive understanding of the legal and regulatory framework. Entrepreneurs should seek professional advice and guidance to ensure compliance with the law and minimize legal risks. By operating within the legal framework, entrepreneurs can establish a solid foundation for their businesses and focus on growth and innovation.

Identifying Your Business Idea
Subchapter: Identifying Your Business Idea

Aspiring Entrepreneurs in India face a multitude of opportunities and challenges while venturing into the world of business. This subchapter aims to guide you through the process of identifying a viable business idea that aligns with your interests, skills, and the Indian market landscape. Whether you aspire to start a tech startup, a sustainable business, a consulting firm, a manufacturing enterprise, or a social enterprise, the following insights will help you kickstart your entrepreneurial journey.

1. **Understand the Indian market:** Before diving into the business world, it is crucial to conduct thorough market research. Study the current trends, consumer behavior, and industry-specific demands in India. Identify gaps and untapped opportunities that you can leverage to create a unique value proposition.

2. **Assess your skills and interests:** Evaluate your own skills, expertise, and interests. What are you passionate about? What are you exceptionally good at? Consider your professional background, education, and subjective experiences. Identifying a business idea that aligns with your abilities and passions will increase your chances of success and fulfillment.

3. **Identify problems and pain points:** Look for problems or challenges that people face in their daily lives. These can range from technological inefficiencies to environmental concerns, or gaps in services. Brainstorm innovative solutions that can address these pain points effectively. Think about how your business idea can provide value, convenience, or efficiency to

potential customers.

4. **Explore emerging trends and technologies:**
   In today's fast-paced world, staying updated with emerging technologies is crucial. Consider the impact of technologies like Artificial Intelligence, blockchain, Internet of Things, or renewable energy sources. Can you leverage these trends to build a business that caters to the evolving needs of the Indian market?

5. **Validate your idea:** Once you have identified a potential business idea, validate it through market surveys, focus groups, or by piloting a small-scale version of your product or service. Seek feedback from potential customers, industry experts, and mentors to refine your concept further. This validation process will help you gauge the viability and demand for your idea.

6. **Evaluate the competition:**
   Analyze the existing competition in your chosen niche. Identify their strengths, weaknesses, and unique selling points. Differentiate your business ideas by offering something distinct, whether it is a better product, superior customer service, or a unique pricing strategy. Understanding your competition will also help you position your business effectively in the market.

By following these steps, aspiring entrepreneurs in India can identify a business idea that aligns with their interests, skills, and the Indian market demands. Remember, innovation and adaptability are key to success in the dynamic Indian business landscape. Stay open to innovative ideas, collaborate with like-minded individuals, and continually refine your business concept to meet the evolving needs of your target audience.

If it is a manufacturing unit, collaborate and interact with your nearest District Industries Centres (DICs) from the State Industries Dept or nearest MSME-DI from Central Government under Ministry of MSME, State Incubators, Accelerators, Tool Rooms,

National Small Industries Co-operation (NSIC), State Entrepreneur Development Institute (IED) and Industrial Associations. This will solve your initial hiccups and in a few months you will have fair ideas and knowledge about the beast which you are going to handle for the next few years.

Please remember as you are anxious to find success through your entrepreneurial journey, similarly each Government official including bankers are having target to find a potential entrepreneur in this country at this point. However, compared to Women and Second-generation entrepreneurs, the journey for the first-generation entrepreneur is more challenging in India unlike other developed countries.

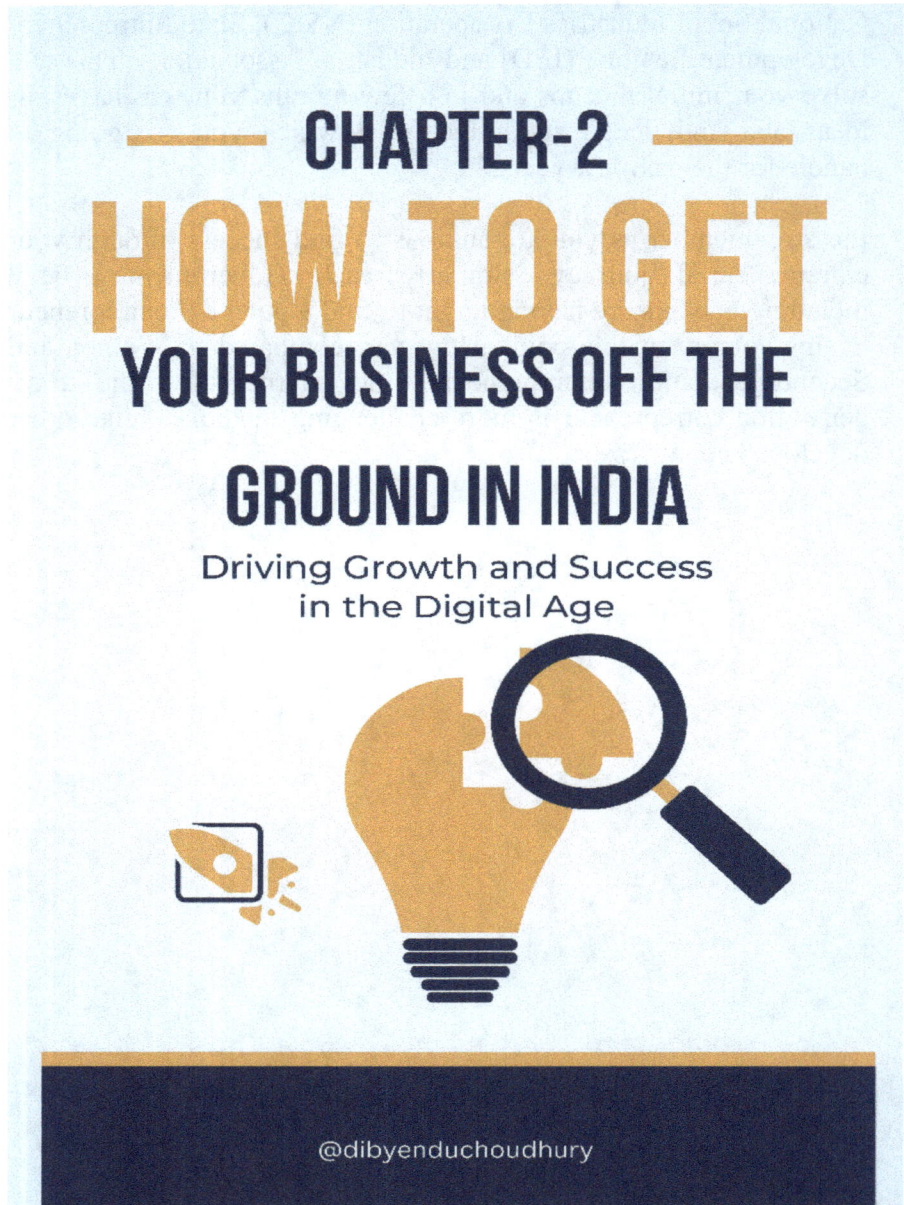

CHAPTER-2

HOW TO GET
YOUR BUSINESS OFF THE
GROUND IN INDIA

Driving Growth and Success in the Digital Age

@dibyenduchoudhury

CHAPTER 2:
HOW TO GET YOUR BUSINESS OFF THE GROUND IN INDIA

Carrying Out Research on the Market in India

When beginning a business in India, conducting market research is one of the most important steps you must take, irrespective of the market segment or sector you intend to operate in. Gaining an understanding of the market as well as the behaviour of consumers is essential for success. Aspiring business owners will find this subchapter to be an invaluable resource, as it details in exhaustive detail how to carry out market research in India.

Finding out who your target demographic should be one of the first things you do while performing market research. It is necessary to segment your target audience based on demographics, geographic area, and psychographics if you are marketing to people in India because India is such a diverse country with a large population. This will enable you to personalize your goods or services to fit their individual requirements and preferences, which will ultimately lead to more sales.

The following phase, after determining your target market, is to collect data and then conduct an analysis of that data. When conducting market research in India, you have a number of different options available to you to choose from. It is possible to obtain information from prospective clients through the use of surveys and questionnaires that can be distributed either online or offline. In addition, qualitative research methods such as interviews and focus groups can provide useful information, enabling you to gain a deeper understanding of the attitudes and motives of customers.

In addition to this, it is essential to keep a close eye on the trends and competitors in the business. The business environment in India is one that is dynamic and constantly changing, notably in the areas of technology startups and consultancy. You can obtain valuable insights into the market and find potential gaps or openings for your company if you study the strategies, products, and pricing employed by your competitors and act accordingly.

In addition, the use of social media platforms in India has become an increasingly vital component of market research. Platforms such as Facebook, Instagram, and Twitter that have a vast user population are able to provide important insights about the behaviour, preferences, and trends of their user base's consumers. You may learn what connects with your target audience and adjust your business accordingly by analyzing the conversations that take place on social media platforms and the material that is generated by users.

In conclusion, when performing market research in India, it is essential to take into account the cultural nuances and local customs that exist there. The culture of this country is extremely rich and varied, and individuals' tastes and preferences might vary greatly from one state or region to another. You will be able to design efficient marketing strategies and interact with your target audience on a deeper level if you can carry out research that takes into account these cultural variables and takes them into account.

To summarize, conducting market research is an essential phase in the process of launching a new business in India. You will be able to make educated judgments that will be important in the success of your business venture in India if you begin by determining your target market, collecting data, analyzing industry trends, keeping an eye on rivals, and taking cultural subtleties into consideration. To understand this part in a simple manner you can even align your business ideas with the major thrust with the Central Government or State Government, out of several studies they have identified the few priority sectors. For an example, right now Central Government entire thrust is to boost the high-performance businesses by implementing and engaging AI, IIOT, Drones, Robots (Industry 4.0). The contemporary ideas e.g., employment of large pool of workforce and social benefits are slowly fading away over more high-tech start-ups which can become Unicorns over short span of time.

The government is also instrumental in creating entrepreneur friendly marketplace and creating to facilitate businesses through Unified Payment Interface (UPI) and Open Network Digital Commerce (ONDC). Transferring money through mobile in a secured manner or Open digital network which is the market of all the marketplaces are not available even in several developed nations. Out of every digital payment in all over the world India made more than 40% in last year. Digital money transfer over mobile phones is adopted and accepted by 80% of the population of India. Imagine a nation of 1.3 Billion population how challenging it is to implement and undertake such daunting tasks.

Developing a Plan for a Business

For any ambitious entrepreneur who is interested in beginning a business in India, developing a business plan is a necessary step in the process. Bankers call it Detailed Business Plan (DPR). You might think of it as a road map that details the objectives, strategies, and financial projections for your company. It doesn't matter if you're launching a social enterprise, a software startup, a sustainable business, a consulting firm, a manufacturing company, or another type of business: having a business plan that's been carefully developed will help you navigate the early phases of your endeavor and make it easier to obtain finance and support.

1. **Making your first step:** Beginning your business plan with a clear and succinct summary of your company's idea, mission, and vision is a good place to start. Bring attention to the one-of-a-kind value proposition that your business

offers, and then quickly describe both your target market and your competitors.

2. **Analyze the Market**: You should do an in-depth study of the industry and market trends that are relevant to your specific specialty. Determine who your target audience is, as well as their requirements and preferences. Conduct a competitive analysis, focusing on how your company will set itself apart from others in the industry.

3. **Product or Service details:** Describe in detail the products or services that you will be making available to customers. Bring your attention to the features and benefits they offer, as well as how they answer the requirements of the market you are trying to reach. Place an emphasis on any novel selling propositions or technological advancements.

4. **Marketing and Sales Strategies:** Outline your marketing and sales strategy here. Marketing and sales strategy go hand in hand. Please explain your pricing strategy, as well as the distribution and promotional activities you have planned. Provide an explanation of how you intend to reach out to potential customers, how you will attract them, and how you will keep them as clients.

5. **Operations and Management:** Please provide a description of the organization of your company, including the key individuals and the legal form it operates under. Describe in detail the operational procedures, the management of the supply chain, and any infrastructural requirements. Bring attention to the talents and experience that your team possesses.

6. **Financial Details**: In your presentation of the financial projections, be sure to include income statements, cash flow statements, and balance sheets. Also, be sure to present an overall financial prognosis. Include the anticipated sales, costs, and profits in your analysis. Include specifics regarding the amount of funding you require as

well as your plans for the investment.

7. **Risk Management and Analysis:** Analyze the various threats and difficulties that your company could be up against as part of your risk assessment and contingency plan. Create a backup plan in case any of these concerns come to pass. This will show potential investors that you have analyzed potential difficulties and have methods in place to overcome them, which is a requirement for attracting their investment.

8. **Additional Supporting Documents:** Include any supporting documents that you feel are necessary, such as market research reports, patents, licenses, or permits in the appendices. In addition, please send the resumes of the important team members, as well as any other pertinent information.

It is important to keep in mind that a business plan is a live document that needs to be continually evaluated and revised as your company moves forward. It ought to be succinct, well-structured, and customized to meet the requirements of your intended audience, whether that audience is composed of potential partners, lenders, or investors.

You will not only have a better grasp of your business idea if you take the time to write out a detailed business plan, but you will also be able to improve your chances of being successful by securing the resources and support you need to make your business idea a reality.

In India, this DPR is considered as the bible for an entrepreneur which reflects his hard work, experiences and passion. You may take help from others while making the DPR, but you must adopt and edit it as per your own document which must reflect your version of the story not others.

Registering Your Business in India

Beginning a new venture in India may be an endeavor that is both thrilling and rewarding. However, before you can venture into the field of entrepreneurship, it is imperative that you have a solid understanding of the steps involved in registering your firm. This subchapter will walk you through the necessary stages involved in registering your business in India and will assist you in navigating the intricate legal landscape that you will encounter here.

1. **Select a Business Structure:** The initial action in the process of establishing your company is to select a business structure that is most appropriate for the nature of your enterprise. The sole proprietorship, partnership, limited liability partnership (LLP), private limited company, and public limited company are the different business structures that are available to choose from in India. Because each structure comes with its own individual set of prerequisites and advantages, it is essential to pick the one that is suitable for achieving the objectives that you have set for your company.

2. **Obtain a Number That Is Exclusively Yours:** Once you have chosen the type of organization your company will take, the next step is to acquire a number that is exclusively yours. Your Permanent Account Number (PAN) will function as your identity number if you operate your business as a sole proprietorship and have Aadhar Number which is a 12-digit unique number. If you are forming a corporation or a partnership, you will be required to register for a one-of-a-kind identification number that will be referred to as the Director Identification Number (DIN) or the Corporate Identification Number (CIN) or even Udyog Aadhar Memorandum (UAM).

3. **Register Your Business with the Registrar of Companies (RoC):** In order to create a legal entity outside of your company, you are required to register your business with the Registrar of Companies (RoC). To complete the registration procedure, you will need to prepare and submit

30

the required documents to the RoC. These will include a Memorandum of Association (MOA) as well as Articles of Association (AOA). It is possible that more documentation will be needed, depending on how your company is structured. For example, in the social sector there are company classification e.g., 80G or Society which are categorized as Non-profit organizations, however their functioning and taxation might be different. Therefore, you must know what you are going for and why.

4. **Obtain the Necessary Licenses and Permits for Your Company:** To conduct business legally in India, certain types of companies are required to possess various licenses and permits. It is of the utmost importance to conduct research, determine which licenses are necessary for your line of work, and then secure those licenses from the relevant authorities. The registration for the Goods and Services Tax (GST), the license to conduct business, the clearance from the environmental agency, and any specialized licenses required for certain industries such as the pharmaceutical or food processing industries are some examples.

5. **Register for Tax Purposes:** If you want your company to follow the Indian tax regulations, you need to register it for taxation purposes. This comprises registering for the Goods and Services Tax (GST), if it is appropriate, and acquiring the requisite licenses for excise duties or customs. Additionally, this includes obtaining a Tax Deduction and Collection Account Number (TAN) for the purpose of deducting and remitting taxes.

6. **Compliance with Employment rules:** If you want to run a successful business in India, it is essential to ensure that you follow the country's employment rules. This entails signing up for the Employees' Provident Fund (EPF), Employee State Insurance (ESI), and Professional Tax (PT), if any of them are necessary. In addition, check to see that you have appropriate employment contracts in place

and that you are abiding by all applicable regulations about working hours, salaries, and benefits.

7. **Continuing to Comply with Ongoing Reporting and Compliance obligations:** Once you have successfully registered with your company, you are required to continue to comply with the ongoing reporting and compliance obligations. This includes complying with any industry-specific rules, filing annual returns, keeping accurate accounting records, and conducting frequent audits.

Keep in mind that registering with your company is simply the first step on the road to becoming a successful entrepreneur. To ensure a seamless and legally compliant beginning process, it is vital to get professional help from lawyers, accountants, and business consultants who are experienced with the Indian business scene. You may lay a solid groundwork for your company in India and get off to a good start as an entrepreneur if you familiarize yourself with the country's registration criteria and do whatever you need to do to satisfy them.

Acquiring Knowledge about Taxation and Obligations

It is essential for you, as an aspiring entrepreneur in India, to familiarize yourself with the complexities of taxation and compliances to successfully navigate the business landscape. This will allow you to successfully navigate the business landscape. In this subchapter, we will delve into the fundamental components of taxation and compliance, giving you the knowledge that is necessary to ensure that your company is following both the law and its financial obligations.

Taxation is an integral part of operating a business in India, and it is critical to have a solid understanding of the many forms of taxation that are imposed on the various sorts of business entities. The Goods and Services Tax (GST), the Income Tax, and the Corporate Tax are the three most popular types of taxes. Each type of tax has its own specific laws and guidelines, and it is imperative that taxpayers adhere to these to avoid incurring penalties and other legal complications. This book will walk you through the fundamentals of each tax and offer advice on how to efficiently handle your tax responsibilities.

Another essential component of launching and operating a business in India is ensuring compliance with local regulations. Compliance guarantees that your company functions within the confines of the legal framework. This might include everything from obtaining the right licenses and permissions to abiding by labour rules. We will provide you with an overview of the many compliance standards that apply to various sorts of organizations, such as social enterprises, sustainable businesses, consulting firms, manufacturing companies, and technology startups, among others. You can safeguard your company and lay strong groundwork for future expansion if you have a good awareness of and adhere to all these compliance standards.

In addition, we will investigate the advantages and possibilities for advancement that are open to commercial enterprises in India. The government encourages business owners to start their own companies by providing them with a variety of incentives, including tax breaks, subsidies, and other forms of financial support. If you have a good knowledge of these opportunities, you will be able to use them to fuel the expansion of your company. In this book I have discussed a few of those opportunities in Chapter 9.

In addition to the legal and financial considerations, we will also talk about the significance of maintaining ethical standards and being responsible in business. It is critical for you, as an entrepreneur, to think about the effects that your company will have on the community and the environment. We will investigate sustainable business practices, initiatives that promote corporate social responsibility, and ethical concerns that can help enhance the reputation of your company and ensure its continued profitability in the long term.

If you have an in-depth grasp of taxation and compliance, you can ensure that your company functions within the confines of the legal system, reduces its exposure to financial risk, and makes a constructive contribution to society. As you prepare to embark on your adventure as an entrepreneur in India, this subchapter will provide you with the information and resources you need to successfully navigate the intricate world of taxes and regulatory compliance. This will set you up for success.

Options Available for Funding and Financing in India

Starting a business in India can be an exciting and rewarding endeavor, but it frequently comes with the obstacle of acquiring the necessary money and financing. Despite this struggle, starting a business in India can be an interesting and rewarding effort. If you are an ambitious entrepreneur with the goal of launching a technology startup, a sustainable business, a consulting firm, a manufacturing company, or a social enterprise, it is essential that you have a solid awareness of the numerous funding alternatives that are accessible in India in order to make your vision a reality.

Venture capital is consistently ranked among the most sought-after methods of financing for new businesses in India. Venture capital organizations make investments in early-stage businesses that have significant potential for expansion. In addition to financial assistance, these companies typically offer strategic direction and connections inside the sector. To be successful in securing money from venture capitalists, entrepreneurs need to have a business plan that is compelling, a business model that is scalable, and a solid team.

Angel investors are yet another possibility for the financing of your company at the early stage. Angel investors are individuals who provide financial assistance to fledgling businesses in exchange for ownership stakes in the company. They frequently make investments in a company at its formative phases, at a time when it may be challenging to obtain traditional capital from other sources. Your prospects of receiving money can be improved by cultivating contacts with angel investors through participation in networking events and communities for startup businesses.

In recent years, crowdfunding has emerged as a viable fundraising alternative for start-up businesses in India, which has contributed to its rise in popularity. Platforms for crowdfunding make it possible for business owners to obtain finance from a substantial number of individuals willing to give only modest sums of money. This alternative not only enables you to obtain financial backing, but it also assists you in validating your business idea and constructing a clientele.

There are government programmes and grants available in India for individuals who are interested in beginning a business that will have a sustainable future. The government of India has launched a number of initiatives to encourage environmentally responsible and sustainable business practices. Entrepreneurs in fields such as organic farming, waste management, and renewable energy can benefit from these programmes by receiving financial support, tax advantages, and technical assistance.

Entrepreneurs in India also have access to conventional finance options like bank loans and company loans from a variety of financial institutions. Banks have a variety of loan programmes that can be customized to meet the particular requirements of new and small businesses. On the other hand, in order to obtain a loan from a bank, you will often need a sound business plan, collateral, and a positive credit history.

In conclusion, if you are thinking about launching a social venture, you should give some thought to impact investors. These investors provide capital to companies that, in addition to generating financial rewards, also have a positive influence on society or the environment. Impact investors are interested in providing financial backing to businesses that work to solve urgent social problems such as poverty, education, and healthcare disparities, as well as climate change.

Government of India at the current stage is one of the largest

Venture capitals to promote entrepreneurship in the country who provides various categories of loans and support through Nationalized Banks and several Govt. Institutions e.g., NSIC provides loans to start-up business for the raw materials and machines. Coir Board and Khadi Village Industries run the largest Govt. Scheme known as employment Generation Programme (PMEGP). SIDBI provides loans for the Services Sector known as MUDRA.

In conclusion, it is necessary for aspiring entrepreneurs across a wide variety of fields to have a solid awareness of the funding and financing choices that are accessible in India. Exploring these many funding alternatives will assist you in securing the resources necessary to transform your idea into a profitable business venture, regardless of whether you are launching a social enterprise, a manufacturing company, a consulting firm, a sustainable business, or a startup in the field of information technology.

CHAPTER-3

HOW TO LAUNCH A SUCCESSFUL TECH STARTUP IN INDIA?

@dibyenduchoudhury

CHAPTER 3: HOW TO LAUNCH A SUCCESSFUL TECH STARTUP IN INDIA

An Overview of the Startup Ecosystem in Indian Technology

Identifying Emerging Trends in India's Technology

In the lightning-fast world of technology, it is absolutely essential for ambitious business owners to stay one step ahead of the competition and recognize the most current trends that have the potential to mould their ideas for businesses. This subchapter aims to provide helpful insights into the technological landscape in India, catering to the diverse niches of starting a business in India, starting a tech startup in India, starting a sustainable business in India, starting a consulting business in India, starting a manufacturing business in India, and starting a social enterprise in India. Specifically, this subchapter will focus on starting a business in India.

India has quickly become a leading player in the global technology industry and thanks to its thriving ecosystem, which encourages innovation and entrepreneurialism. The country has seen a rapid digital transition, which has been spurred by factors such as the increasing prevalence of the Internet, the use of smartphones, and efforts taken by the government such as Digital India initiative. These trends can be used to an aspiring entrepreneur's advantage in order to develop successful firms.

The growth of e-commerce is one of the most notable developments in technological trends in India. The rapid expansion of online shopping can be attributed to a large global population as well as the expanding availability of the Internet. Entrepreneurs

38

have the opportunity to capitalize on this trend by building e-commerce platforms, delivering one-of-a-kind goods or services, or coming up with novel solutions to the problems that are now being experienced by online retailers.

The implementation of artificial intelligence (AI) and machine learning (ML) is another key trend that has emerged recently. Because it has such a large pool of skilled engineers and data scientists, India is a perfect location for organizations that are focused on artificial intelligence and machine learning. Opportunities for business growth can be found in areas such as healthcare, banking, agriculture, and education, all of which could benefit from the revolutionary and time-saving effects of artificial intelligence (AI).

In addition, the concept of sustainability has emerged as a fundamental concern for companies operating in India. The nation is making efforts to lessen its overall carbon footprint and increase the use of renewable energy sources. Aspiring business owners who are interested in capitalizing on this trend might do so by creating environmentally friendly products, providing sustainable solutions, or incorporating sustainable business practices into their operational models.

The consulting industry in India provides numerous options for company owners to start their own companies and deliver specialized services to commercial clients. As a result of the expansion of the economy, businesses need specialized knowledge in fields such as market research, digital marketing, financial planning, and the formulation of strategies. Entrepreneurs have the ability to build consulting firms that cater to the specific requirements of businesses, thereby providing those organizations with vital insights and direction.

The "Make in India" campaign that India is currently running has produced a favourable climate for those who are interested in the manufacturing industry. The government has implemented a number of different reforms and incentives in order to encourage indigenous manufacturing and minimize reliance on imported goods. The major thrust is on "Make in India and Made in India," "Zero Defect and Zero Effect (ZED)," Intellectual Property Rights (IPR) and recently on Raising and accelerating the MSME Performances (RAMP). Those looking to start their own businesses can find markets that have a strong demand and then construct manufacturing units there. To improve their output, efficiency and performance they can utilize high-end technology such as automation and robotics.

In conclusion, the concept of social entrepreneurship has been gaining tremendous traction in India. Innovative business models give entrepreneurs the opportunity to direct their attention towards the resolution of urgent societal problems. This can include empowering groups who have been historically marginalized and supporting sustainable practices. Providing access to education, healthcare, or clean water are also examples of this. Entrepreneurs have the opportunity to make a beneficial impact on society while also developing successful enterprises if they take on social issues. Micro Finance Companies run by Self Help Groups (SHGs) and gaining momentum in India. Kudumbashree, Lizzat, Patanjali, ITC e-Choupal are the few names with AMUL which are very well-known companies in the Social Sector.

Government of India undertakes Cluster Development activities to make the unorganized sector more organized by forming Special purpose vehicles (SPVs). There are several funding opportunities are there e.g., SFURTI for the traditional arts, crafts and handloom sectors vis-à-vis cluster development programme (CDP) for large cluster development. There are several initiatives to establish Common Facility Centres (CFCs), Infrastructure Development and even Multi-product Cluster Development Approach.

To summarize, it is essential for aspiring business owners in India to be aware of the many technological developments. Entrepreneurs can leverage the potential of e-commerce, artificial intelligence, sustainability, consultancy, manufacturing, and social entrepreneurship to establish firms that are successful and have an influence on the world if they have a solid understanding of the ever-changing environment of the technology industry.

Opportunities in India's technology sector are unbounded when approached with the appropriate level of expertise and level of strategic planning.

Developing a Skilled Workforce in India

Building a tech workforce that is capable of doing their jobs well is one of the most important parts of creating a successful tech firm in India. Aspiring business owners in a nation renowned for its thriving technological ecosystem need to have a solid grasp on how to entice and keep the best employees if they want to be successful. This subchapter will provide insightful information on how to construct a tech team in India, with a particular focus on meeting the requirements of those who are considering launching a firm in the technology sector.

The pool of technical expertise in India is extensive and varied, and it offers a wide variety of qualified experts. However, it is absolutely necessary to have a well-thought-out plan in place in order to locate and entice the appropriate people to join your team. The first thing you need to do is determine the roles that need to be filled and the skill sets that are necessary for your startup. Understanding the exact expertise required can help you target the ideal individuals, whether you need User Interface and User Experience (UI/UX) designers, data scientists, or software developers. Understanding the specific knowledge is essential.

In India, the process of hiring new employees frequently incorporates a combination of modern and traditional methods. The usage of employment portals and other Internet platforms is common, but networking and word of mouth also play a crucial role in the hiring process. You may tap into the talent pool and identify the ideal people for your team by establishing connections with local IT groups, attending industry events, and making use of social media platforms.

When it comes to developing a tech team in India, cultural compatibility is just as important as technical expertise. The

41

importance of cooperation, teamwork, and close personal connections are highly valued by Indians. When conducting interviews with potential employees, it is important to assess their teamwork skills as well as their capacity to adjust to the fast-paced environment of a startup.

After you have put together your IT team, the next most major step is to cultivate an atmosphere that encourages creative thinking and professional advancement. It is possible to recruit and keep top personnel by providing possibilities for professional development, flexible working hours, and pay that is competitive in the market. In addition, increasing the sense of community and support inside the workplace will lead to increased levels of contentment and productivity among staff members.

The process of putting together a technological team in India is not without its obstacles. The competition for qualified professionals can be intense, and keeping hold of such professionals can be a challenging endeavor. Aspiring entrepreneurs may, however, develop a strong tech team that will propel their firm toward success by gaining an awareness of the local tech industry, utilizing a variety of recruitment tactics, and cultivating an inclusive work environment.

This section is useful not just for those interested in launching a technology-based company, but also for business owners investigating opportunities in other fields, such as consulting, manufacturing, social enterprises, and sustainable companies. In the modern digital age, where technology is the primary driver of innovation and competitiveness, having a strong tech team is essential in any business, regardless of the industry. Aspiring business owners who are familiar with the intricacies of assembling a technological team in India are in a better position to achieve success in the industry of their choice and to successfully navigate the challenges associated with launching a company in India provided they have good connectivity with the market and have few clients in their hands.

It is advisable that any business is good for India provided you have few steady orders in your hands to sustain for some time and figure out the ways slowly. Today only order supplying or even traders are recognized as entrepreneurs and start-ups. Financial Institutions are eager to fund the entrepreneurs who have standing orders in their hands. Establishing your own brand might take a long time, therefore sustenance is the mantra to be a successful entrepreneur.

Legal Protections for Intellectual Property and Related Matters

Aspiring business owners need to give thoughtful consideration to intellectual property rights in order to be successful in today's fast-paced and intensely competitive business environment. Understanding the relevance of intellectual property rights and how to safeguard them is necessary before beginning your path to start a business in India. As you embark on this journey, it is important to grasp the significance of intellectual property rights. This subchapter will walk you through the numerous facets of intellectual property rights in India, providing you with the information to protect your ideas, innovations, and creations. The goal is to make this subchapter as useful to you as possible.

To begin with the fundamentals, intellectual property is the term used to describe the intangible assets that are created through the application of human intelligence. Inventions, trademarks, copyrights, industrial designs, and trade secrets are all included in this category. These assets are frequently the driving force behind a company's success and serve as the basis around which it is built. It is considered as intangible asset for an organization and creates larger valuations. As a result, it is absolutely necessary to acquire the knowledge necessary to safeguard and preserve your intellectual property.

Legal protections for intellectual property are quite well-developed on the Indian subcontinent. It is important for you, as an aspiring entrepreneur, to be informed about the assorted options for protecting your intellectual property that are accessible. For instance, if you have developed an original piece of software or method, you should think about filing for a patent on your creation. This will offer you exclusive rights for a certain period of time to exploit your idea in a business capacity. In a similar vein, trademarks protect the identity of your brand, copyrights protect your creative works, and industrial designs secure the outward appearance of your items. All of these protect the entrepreneur from counterfeit products or copyright infringements and ultimately provide the entry barriers for other businesses to enter into the same business.

However, merely acquiring rights to intellectual property is not sufficient on its own. In addition to this, you need to take preventative measures to safeguard them against infringement. This subchapter will give you actionable techniques to protect your intellectual property, such as conducting regular audits, monitoring the market for potential infringements, and taking appropriate legal action when it becomes necessary to do so.

In addition, the significance of licensing agreements and the ways in which these agreements can be utilized to increase the value of your intellectual property will be discussed in this subchapter. You are able to grant other people permission to use your intellectual property in exchange for royalties or other types of compensation by means of the licensing process. If you are able to navigate the complexities of licensing agreements, you will be in a better position to form mutually beneficial relationships and broaden the scope of your company.

In the final part of this lesson, we will discuss the international implications of intellectual property rights and how they can affect your company. Because of the increasing globalization of markets, it is essential to have a solid understanding of the intricate web of international intellectual property rules and treaties in order to safeguard your assets outside the boundaries of India.

Understanding and safeguarding your intellectual property rights is essential if you are beginning any kind of business, whether it be a social enterprise, a manufacturing venture, a consulting firm, a sustainable business, or a startup in the technology industry. This subchapter will provide you with the information and resources necessary to negotiate the complexities of intellectual property rights in India, thereby assuring the long-term success and viability of your company as well as safeguarding the Unique Selling Propositions (USP) for your company.

Implementing Growth Strategies for Your Tech Startup in India

Aspiring entrepreneurs who are interested in starting a business in India, particularly in the technology industry, need to have a solid understanding of the one-of-a-kind opportunities and challenges that come with scaling and growing a technology firm in this country. The IT startup ecosystem in India has emerged as one of the most rapidly expanding in the world, presenting enormous potential for business owners who are able to efficiently manage the environment.

The journey from Micro to Small is the biggest challenge because the most daunting part in the business is to scale-up. Managing the scale through professionals is the next level of challenge. The majority of the Micro enterprise die during infancy stage because they are not managed well. When trying to scale-up your software firm in India, one of the most important considerations to make is the country's massive and varied market. India has a population that is greater than 1.3 billion people, making it a vast consumer base that is ravenous for cutting-edge technological solutions. However, it is essential to have a solid understanding of the intricacies of the Indian market, such as the tastes of different regions, the richness of Indian culture, and the digital divide that exists between urban and rural areas. However, the urban and rural divide is diminishing amazingly fast in India due to high rate of digital literacy and adoption. Also, one of the most impeding factors of digital adoption in India because of its majority of the population is young and literate. It will be essential to your company's success if you modify and match your product or service to attract this segment.

Building a powerful team is another critical issue to concentrate on. In India, there is a vast pool of competent tech professionals waiting to be recruited, and it is essential to scale your firm by recruiting and retaining the proper staff. Invest in the creation of a positive work culture, provide chances for growth and skill development, and offer competitive compensation packages. Working together with nearby academic institutions and technological communities can also help you tap into the available talent pool.

When it comes to expanding a digital startup's operations, having access to finance is one of the most crucial factors. In recent years, India has witnessed a tremendous surge in venture capital and angel investments, presenting business owners with a wide variety of options to choose from when it comes to securing money. Having said that, it is essential to have a business strategy that is well-defined, an elevator pitch that is engaging, and a comprehensive awareness of the landscape of investors in India. You can increase your chances of successfully raising the necessary funds by cultivating relationships with investors, participating in startup events, and making use of government initiatives such as Startup or Standup India. You can even get incubated in State funded incubators during the early stage.

In addition, expanding your tech startup's operations to a larger scale in India may need you to form strategic relationships and collaborate with other businesses. Find suitable partners, both inside and outside of the tech industry, who can complement your product or service and help you reach a wider audience. This can be done by identifying potential partners. Working together with well-established businesses, business incubators and accelerators, as well as government organizations, can enable significant growth with crucial support and resources. Even that will show you the opportunities to find the early-stage funding.

In conclusion, if your digital startup is looking for a competitive advantage, integrating sustainability and social impact may be the way to go. The concepts of sustainability and social entrepreneurship are gaining more and more attention in India. Not only may incorporating sustainable practices, such as employing renewable energy sources or implementing eco-friendly manufacturing techniques, help you cut expenses, but they can also attract customers and investors who are socially conscious.

Growing and scaling a technology firm in India is an exciting adventure that is full of chances and obstacles. Aspiring entrepreneurs should position themselves for success in this dynamic ecosystem by gaining a grasp of the Indian market, forming a dedicated team, acquiring capital, establishing strategic relationships, and embracing sustainability.

CHAPTER - 4

HOW TO ESTABLISH
A PROFITABLE AND LASTING
BUSINESS IN INDIA

SUSTAINABLE BUSINESS

The term "sustainability" refers to the ability to meet existing demands without compromising the ability of future generations to meet their own needs.

@DIBYENDUCHOUDHURY

CHAPTER 4: HOW TO ESTABLISH A PROFITABLE AND LASTING BUSINESS IN INDIA

Acquiring an Awareness of the Significance of Sustainability in India

India has become one of the most attractive destinations for business owners who are wanting to launch a new venture as a result of the country's fast-expanding economy and quickly expanding population. Despite this, there is a pressing need to address the environmental and social concerns that come hand-in-hand with this growth. In recent years, sustainability has become an increasingly vital component in determining the success and longevity of enterprises in India. This subchapter's goal is to shed light on the significance of sustainability and its consequences for aspiring entrepreneurs in a variety of sectors, such as beginning a tech company, a sustainable business, a consultancy firm, a manufacturing business, or a social enterprise in India. Specifically, the subchapter will focus on the relevance of sustainability and its implications for aspiring entrepreneurs in India.

The term "sustainability" refers to the ability to meet existing demands without compromising the ability of future generations to meet their own needs. This is the essence of what it means to be sustainable. In the context of India, it refers to a wide range of concerns, such as the protection of the natural environment, the fulfillment of social responsibilities, and the maintenance of economic security. Understanding sustainability principles and incorporating them into company practices is no longer a desirable option for business owners in India; rather, it has become an absolute requirement.

The rising level of consciousness and concern over the deterioration of the environment is one of the primary forces that is fueling the rising importance of sustainable practices. India is up against enormous environmental issues, including pollution of the air and water, loss of forest cover, and the effects of climate change. Entrepreneurs have a responsibility to acknowledge that the actions they conduct have both direct and indirect effects on the environment and to take preventative measures in order to reduce the amount of ecological damage they cause.

In addition, sustainability involves not just issues pertaining to the environment but also those pertaining to society and the economy as well. Entrepreneurs have a responsibility to acknowledge the significance of social responsibility in the operations of their businesses, which includes tackling issues such as gender equality, fair labour practices, and community development. In addition, developing a sustainable company strategy can increase long-term profitability, which is important considering the growing demand from customers for goods and services that are in line with their own beliefs and ideals.

Aspiring businesspeople who want to launch a technology startup can easily incorporate environmentally friendly practices into the core of their company's business strategy. Tech businesses have the potential to generate a beneficial effect while simultaneously boosting revenue if they leverage technology to offer innovative solutions to serious environmental and social concerns.

In a similar vein, individuals who want to build their own businesses in the consulting sector can provide clients with advice on sustainable practices, green supply chain, guiding them through the maze of sustainability legislation and initiatives that exist in India. Consultants can present themselves as beneficial partners for firms that are working to become more sustainable if they offer specialized knowledge and expertise in the field of sustainability.

In the manufacturing industry, achieving sustainability can be accomplished by implementing production methods that are less harmful to the environment, maximizing the use of available resources, and maintaining ethical supplier networks. This not only lessens our impact on the surrounding environment, but it also improves our operational efficacy and our cost-effectiveness.

Last but not least, businesspeople who are interested in launching a social company can tap into the strength of business to find solutions to problems in the social and natural environments. Social enterprises are businesses that combine profit-making operations with a social mission in order to generate solutions that are both sustainable and scalable and that are to benefit underserved communities and the environment.

In summing up, sustainability has evolved into an extremely crucial factor for entrepreneurs to take into account across a wide range of industries in India. Aspiring entrepreneurs in India may develop successful, impactful, and future-proof enterprises that generate positive change in the country by first gaining an awareness of the significance of sustainability and then adopting it into their business practices.

The Identification of Viable Business Opportunities in India

Aspiring business owners who want to launch a company that will be successful will find a wealth of chances to pursue in India as a result of the country's dynamic economy and the broad market. In this subchapter, we will investigate the many different paths and subfields that offer excellent opportunities for people who desire to have a beneficial effect on the environment and society while also creating income for themselves.

To successfully launch a long-term enterprise in India, one must have a comprehensive knowledge of the specific opportunities and obstacles that are presented by the nation. The field of renewable energy is one of the most important arenas in which sustainable enterprises have a chance to flourish. There is a significant amount of opportunity for business owners to tap into this market in India, given the country's lofty goal of obtaining 40% of its energy from renewable sources by the year 2030. There is a growing demand for innovative solutions to meet India's energy needs in a manner that is sustainable. Some examples of such solutions include solar power, wind energy, Hydrogen and biofuels.

51

Another market segment that merits investigation is the waste management industry. Every day, India produces a substantial amount of waste, and conventional approaches to garbage disposal are no longer viable options. This presents an opportunity for business owners to capitalize on the market by creating novel approaches to trash management, such as recycling, composting, or the generation of energy from waste products. These enterprises not only contribute to the elimination of environmental pollution but also make new job openings available to the people in the surrounding community.

In addition to that, the sector of social enterprise in India is expanding at a rapid rate. If you are an aspiring entrepreneur with the dual goals of making a positive impact on society and running a successful business, you will discover that industries such as healthcare, education, and agriculture offer enormous prospects. For instance, establishing low-cost healthcare clinics in rural areas, constructing educational platforms (EdTech) driven by technology, and promoting organic farming(Aggrotech) practices are all activities that can have a real influence on the lives of people while also providing stable earnings.

Opportunities can be found in India not just in the fields of renewable energy, waste management, and social enterprises, but also in the fields of technology startup firms, consultancy businesses, and manufacturing businesses. Both the technology and industrial sectors are well positioned for expansion as a result of the government's initiatives to promote digitalization and the "Make in India" campaign. In India, business owners who have experience in the aforementioned fields can capitalize on their talents and knowledge to launch and grow prosperous enterprises. Only in the year 2020, there had been 1500 Aggrotech start-ups came in the market who are having different focus on Agri sector e.g., Robotics, Drones, Cloud, High tech Irrigation systems, Finance or even lending businesses to FPO's. Beyond 2030 the Aggrotech companies will focus on reducing the waste in this sector. A few names e.g., Kishan Raja, Dhanuka Aggrotech, Gofers are already there.

To be successful in locating profitable business prospects in India, one must have a sharp eye for difficulties and a powerful desire to make a constructive contribution. Aspiring business owners can create profitable and meaningful operations that contribute to India's sustainable development while also reaping financial advantages if they take the time to gain an awareness of the specific requirements of the Indian market and take advantage of developing trends.

Understanding the sustainable business opportunities in India is key to realizing your entrepreneurial goals. Whether you are interested in creating a software company, consultancy business, manufacturing organization, or social enterprise, understanding the sustainable business prospects in India is essential. You will gain the insights and knowledge required to successfully navigate the Indian business landscape and contribute to a more sustainable future by reading this subchapter. These insights and expertise will allow you to successfully recognize and capitalize on opportunities that present themselves.

Introducing Environmentally Responsible Policies into Your Company

In the modern world, sustainability has evolved into an essential component of the success of businesses. Aspiring entrepreneurs in India need to understand the significance of incorporating environmentally conscious policies and procedures into their enterprise models. Not only will businesses be contributing to the preservation of the environment, but they will also be appealing to a growing market of consumers who are environmentally sensitive if they take these steps. In this subchapter, we will examine the primary measures that need to be taken in order to implement sustainable practices in your company, independent of the market sector that you operate in.

1. **Conduct a Sustainability Audit:** It is vital for your company to evaluate its current level of environmental

effect before beginning the implementation of sustainable practices. Conduct an exhaustive audit of your company's sustainability practices in order to determine the areas in which it can make improvements. This may involve the consumption of energy, the management of trash, the use of water, and the emissions of carbon.

2. **Identification of Sector/Area:** After you have determined the areas in which your company could develop, the next step is to formulate long-term objectives for your company that are both detailed and measurable. These objectives will serve as a road map for your path towards sustainability and will keep you focused on generating results that can be seen and touched. Think about setting goals such as lowering your overall energy consumption by a specific percentage or starting a recycling initiative.

3. **Adopting Renewable Energy:** Adopting renewable energy sources is one of the most efficient methods to lessen the impact that your company has on the environment, and it is also one of the most environmentally friendly things that your company can do. Investigate environmentally beneficial alternatives to conventional energy sources such as solar power, wind energy, and others. Additionally, to cut down on your usage of electricity, you can think about purchasing energy-efficient equipment and lighting.

4. **Implement Waste Reduction Strategies:** Evaluate the practices your company employs for waste management and determine ways to cut down on the amount of waste that is generated. Encourage people to recycle and take into consideration establishing a composting programme. Investigate possible replacements for plastics that are used just once and urge the companies who supply you to adopt environmentally responsible packaging practices.

5. **Green Supply Chain:** Assessing your supply chain and forming partnerships with suppliers and manufacturers who place a priority on sustainability are both important steps in

promoting sustainable supply chains. Choose vendors who are committed to upholding ethical standards and protecting the environment in their business practices. You are making a contribution to the long-term viability of your sector as a whole when you advocate for sustainable supply chains.

6. **Educate and Involve Employees:** The first step in developing a culture of sustainability within your organization is to focus on the employees themselves. You should provide your staff with education on the significance of environmentally responsible practices and urge them to take an active role in your organization's efforts to promote sustainability. Encourage a sense of environmental responsibility by instituting procedures in the workplace that are less harmful to the environment.

7. **Environmental Responsibility:** After you have put sustainable practices into place, it is important to convey your efforts to preserve the environment to the people you are trying to influence. Bring attention to your company's dedication to environmental responsibility by highlighting it in marketing campaigns, on social media platforms, and on its website. This will pique the interest of environmentally conscious customers whose beliefs are congruent with yours.

You will not only be making a contribution to a greener future by incorporating sustainable practices into your company, but you will also be enhancing the reputation of your brand and increasing its attractiveness to a rising market of consumers who are environmentally conscious. Keep in mind that sustainability is not a one-time effort but rather an ongoing commitment to protect our planet for the generations that will come after us. Take on the challenge and ensure that your company's operations in India are sustainable by making it a priority.

Developing Sustainable Partnerships and Working Relationships for the Environment

In the linked world of today, developing alliances and working together on projects is absolutely necessary for the success and continued existence of any organization. This subchapter examines the significance of establishing solid partnerships and provides actionable advice on how to initiate, cultivate, and sustain these associations within the context of the Indian commercial environment. This section will provide essential insights that will help you manage the intricacies of collaboration, whether you are an ambitious entrepreneur in India trying to create a tech startup, a sustainable business, a consultancy firm, a manufacturing business, or a social enterprise. These insights will help you negotiate the complexities of cooperation.

Startups and established companies in India can gain a great deal from forming strategic alliances and working together on projects. They can give you access to new markets, resources, specialist knowledge, and prospects for funding, all of which are necessary for growth and sustainability. Entrepreneurs who collaborate with individuals, organizations, and institutions that have similar goals might benefit from the sharing of knowledge and networks, thereby lowering their operating expenses and expanding their customer base. In addition, commercial alliances make it possible for companies to capitalize on the combined capabilities of a number of different entities, which in turn encourages innovation and boosts competitiveness.

Aspiring business owners should begin the process of building effective partnerships and collaborations by locating possible partners whose core beliefs, long-term goals, and areas of expertise are congruent with their desired outcomes for their companies. Connecting with possible collaborators can be facilitated through a number of beneficial resources, including Internet platforms, industry conferences, and networking events. It is absolutely necessary to carry out in-depth research in order to have an understanding of the possible partner's track record, reputation, and the degree to which it is compatible with your business strategy.

When possible, business partners have been located, the next step is to write agreements that are transparent and advantageous to both parties. This includes laying down the allocation of resources, risks, and rewards, as well as describing the roles, responsibilities, and expectations of each of the parties engaged in the transaction. Communication that is open and honest must take place at all times during the partnership in order to cultivate trust and reduce disagreements.

In addition, business owners should be actively on the lookout for opportunities to share knowledge and skills, as well as to collaborate on the resolution of issues. Workshops, seminars, and mentorship programmes are examples of collaborative projects that can allow the interchange of ideas and experiences, thereby establishing an environment that is supportive of the growth of businesses in a sustainable manner.

In conclusion, forming strategic alliances and working cooperatively with other businesses is an essential tactic for ambitious business owners in India who wish to launch and maintain a profitable enterprise. Entrepreneurs have the ability to overcome problems, gain access to new markets, and propel innovation when they leverage the capabilities, networks, and resources of partners. It is important to keep in mind that the foundations of successful collaborations include identifying partners who share your vision and values, having explicit agreements, and encouraging open communication. Embrace the power of partnerships on your journey towards becoming an entrepreneur, and you will unleash the possibilities for development and sustainability.

Assessing and Disseminating the Effects Your Sustainable Business Has

Due to the fast-shifting nature of the modern business landscape, the concept of sustainability has emerged as a crucial consideration for new business owners and startup companies in India. It is absolutely necessary for you, as an aspiring entrepreneur, to have a solid understanding of how to measure and convey the impact of your sustainable business. The purpose of this subchapter is to function as a guide for you throughout the process, providing insightful information as well as helpful hints and guidelines that will assist you in demonstrating the beneficial effects that your endeavour has had on the environment and the community.

It is crucial for your sustainable business to measure the impact that it has for a number of reasons. To begin, it enables you to assess how far along you are in the process of attaining your sustainability goals and to make decisions that are informed by data in order to enhance your business practices. Second, it offers transparency to your stakeholders, including as investors, consumers, and employees, who are increasingly looking for companies that have a social and environmental conscience and value those companies more. Last but not least, evaluating impact enables you to measure your performance against the standards of your sector and locate areas in which you may make improvements.

To accurately quantify the impact of your company, you must first establish sustainability goals that are both specific and quantitative. These objectives ought to be harmonized with the Sustainable Development Goals (SDGs) of the United Nations or with any other applicable frameworks that tackle particular social or environmental problems. After you have decided what you want to accomplish, the next step is to select key performance indicators (KPIs) that will show how far you have come toward achieving your objectives. Metrics such as lowering the company's carbon footprint, professionally managing trash, ensuring the health and safety of employees, and actively participating in the community could fall into this category.

When it comes to gauging impact, collecting correct data is really necessary. Install tracking and monitoring tools and systems to ensure that relevant data points are consistently tracked and monitored. Utilizing technological solutions, carrying out frequent audits, or forming partnerships with specialized organizations that can aid in the collection and analysis of data are all potential steps in this direction. If you have access to trustworthy data, you will be in a better position to recognize patterns, assess how well you have performed over time, and convey the significance of your work to others.

It is of equal importance to communicate the impact that your sustainable business is having. Building trust, attracting investors, and differentiating your brand in a crowded market are all made possible as a result of this capability. To get started, construct an engaging story that focuses on the good change that is being brought about by your company. Make use of tactics from the art of storytelling to captivate your audience and make the impact more relatable.

Reaching out to multiple stakeholders requires making use of a variety of communication channels, such as your website, social media, and more traditional forms of media. Please feel free to share any success stories, case studies, or testimonials that illustrate the tangible benefits that have resulted from your sustainable practices. Think about forming strategic alliances with influential people or people who are considered to be thought leaders in the field of sustainability so that you may spread your message further.

In addition, you should think about getting certifications or accreditations from a third party so that your sustainability claims may be validated. These certifications can demonstrate to your stakeholders and bring credibility to your company at the same time. They also show that your company is complying with standards that are recognized within its sector.

As a conclusion, for aspiring business owners in India, it is crucial to understand how to measure and communicate the impact of your sustainable business. Not only will you be able to attract clients and investors, but you will also be able to contribute to a more sustainable future if you establish distinct goals, collect accurate data, and successfully communicate your accomplishments. You can gain a competitive advantage in the Indian market by adopting sustainability as a fundamental principle for your company and putting that principle into practice.

CHAPTER-5

HOW TO GET YOUR CONSULTING BUSINESS OFF THE GROUND IN INDIA

Driving Growth and Success
in the Digital Age

@DIBYENDUCHOUDHURY

CHAPTER 5: HOW TO GET YOUR CONSULTING BUSINESS OFF THE GROUND IN INDIA

An Explanation of the Indian Consulting Industry

In recent years, the industry of consulting in India has experienced amazing growth, and as a result, it has become an important contributor to the economy of the country. This section provides an overview of the consulting sector and highlights significant aspects that would-be business owners in India should think about before launching a consulting firm.

The consulting industry in India is characterized by a varied range of services catering to numerous industries, such as technology, finance, healthcare, marketing, and human resources. These are only a few of the areas that the industry serves. Consulting companies in India provide knowledge in a variety of areas, including the design of strategies, the improvement of company processes, market research, financial analysis and more. There is a growing demand for consulting services to assist organizations in navigating complex challenges and achieving sustainable growth as a result of the constantly changing business landscape in the country.

The rise in the number of new ventures and businesses in their initial stages that are interested in obtaining expert advice is one of the primary forces behind the expansion of the consulting industry in India. Aspiring business owners can benefit from the knowledge and experience of consultants when formulating business strategies, developing plans for entering new markets, and improving operational efficiency. Consultants also play an important part in supporting established businesses in areas such as mergers and acquisitions, organizational restructuring, and digital transformation, all of which are examples of areas where transformation is necessary.

A huge rise in demand has been observed in India for services related to technology and digital consulting. There is a significant need for consultants who specialize in fields such as data analytics, artificial intelligence, cloud computing, and cybersecurity as a result of the government's push toward digitalization and the rise of technology-driven companies. This expanding market is an opportunity for entrepreneurs who are interested in the digital transformation journey of India to contribute to that journey by starting a technology firm or providing technical consultancy services.

In addition, the consulting sector in India has seen significant growth in the field of sustainability consulting, making it a prominent niche within the industry. Businesses are looking for more direction on how to implement sustainable practices, how to reduce their carbon footprint, and how to comply with legislation as a direct result of the country's increased emphasis on sustainable development and environmental protection. Consulting firms that steer businesses towards environmentally responsible and socially conscious practices can be established as a business venture by enterprising individuals with a passion for sustainable practices.

It is vital to take into consideration a number of criteria before to launching a consulting firm in India. These include having a grasp of the demand in the market, determining who your target demographic is, constructing a solid network of relationships within the business, and getting the appropriate skills and certifications. In addition, business owners need to be aware of the regulatory and legal requirements that must be met, such as obtaining all of the appropriate licenses and registrations.

In summing up, those who are interested in starting their own businesses will find that the consulting industry in India has enormous potential. Entrepreneurs can successfully build consulting businesses that cater to the varied demands of Indian organizations if they have an awareness of the dynamics of the market, a focus on new niches, and a commitment to staying current with trends in the sector.

Finding Your Sweet Spot in the Consulting World

Finding your specific area of expertise is essential to distinguishing yourself in the competitive world of business and realizing your full potential. When it comes to launching a successful consulting practice in India, this observation holds just as much water. Aspiring business owners need to be aware that consulting is a diverse industry, and that specializing in a particular subfield can help them carve out a distinct place for themselves in the market.

How to Get Your Business Off the Ground in India

It is crucial, while beginning a consulting firm in India, to determine your specialty based on your area of expertise and the things that you are passionate about. Take into consideration the fields or markets in which you have previous experience and the areas in which your expertise can be most beneficial. Are you well-versed in marketing strategies? Do you have any experience working in the fields of human resources or finance? Determine your consulting niche by first determining your areas of expertise and your areas of interest.

How to Get Your Own Tech Startup Off the Ground in India

The information and communications technology sector in India is seeing phenomenal growth, which has opened up a wealth of prospects for consultants working in the field. You have many options available to you if you want to become a consultant for tech startups, including specializing in software development, cybersecurity, artificial intelligence, or digital marketing. You may establish yourself as an authority in a certain area of the technology industry if you limit your expertise and offer customized solutions to businesses that are struggling.

How to Get Your Foot in the Door of a Viable Business in India.

64

As the emphasis on sustainability and environmental responsibility continues to expand, aspiring company owners in India who are interested in capitalizing on this trend have the opportunity to do so by launching a consultancy business that is focused on sustainability. This specialized field may involve advising businesses on environmentally friendly practices, assisting those businesses in obtaining certifications or directing those businesses through the process of transitioning into environmentally conscious organizations. You will be able to attract clients who are socially concerned and make a contribution to a greener future if you match your consulting services with sustainable practices.

How to Get Your Consulting Firm Off the Ground in India

Beginning a consulting firm in India demands careful evaluation of the knowledge you bring to the table as well as the clientele you intend to serve. Do you have experience in the fields of management consulting, finance consulting, or perhaps even information technology consulting? Finding your specific area of expertise within the field of consulting will enable you to set yourself apart from other consultants and provide specialized services that are tailored to the requirements of individual customers.

How to Get Your Manufacturing Company Off the Ground in India

It is possible to make a lot of money by beginning a consulting business in the industrial sector if you have previous experience in this field. If you have experience working as a manufacturing consultant, you will be able to guide business owners through the challenging procedure of establishing a manufacturing company in India. This may involve providing guidance on the establishment of a factory, the management of supply chains, quality control, or regulatory compliance. By specializing in this one particular subfield, you will establish yourself as a knowledgeable authority in the manufacturing sector and be in a position to offer insightful advice to prospective business owners.

How to Get a Social Business Off the Ground in India

Those who are enthusiastic about having a constructive influence on society may find that launching a consultancy business in the area of social enterprise may be an extremely gratifying endeavour. Working as a social enterprise consultant allows you to focus on assisting organizations in the process of developing economically viable business models that also address societal or environmental challenges. This may involve advice on various funding alternatives, the measurement of impact, or strategic cooperation opportunities. You will be able to use your experience to advise and guide budding social entrepreneurs in India if you first determine your area of specialization within social entrepreneurship.

In conclusion, when beginning a firm in India, it is essential to determine the specific consulting field in which you will operate. Whether you want to concentrate on a particular sector of the economy or a social issue, identifying your niche enables you to distinguish yourself from the competition, deliver specialized services, and bring in customers who value the expertise you bring to the table. You can thrive in the competitive Indian business scene by recognizing your own talents and interests in addition to the requirements of your target market. This will allow you to present yourself as a trustworthy consultant.

Creating a Consulting Strategy and Process Framework and Methodology

If you are considering entering the field of entrepreneurship, having a consulting framework and process that is well defined can significantly increase your chances of being successful. In this subchapter, we will delve into the most important parts of establishing a consulting framework and methodology that is uniquely adapted to the business landscape of India. This guide will give you essential ideas and techniques, regardless of whether you want to create a software company, a sustainable business, a consultancy firm, a manufacturing business, or a social enterprise.

1. **Having a Solid Understanding** of the Indian Business Environment It is essential, prior to establishing your consulting framework, to have a solid understanding of the distinctive features that make up the Indian business environment. Learn about the regulatory requirements, cultural nuances, market trends, and competitive factors that shape the Indian market so that you can successfully compete there. To effectively modify your framework, conduct an in-depth study on the market and keep yourself apprised of the most recent advancements in the industry.

2. **Determine Your Target Market:** Determine your target market based on the specific niche you intend to serve, such as the technology industry, environmentally friendly practices, consulting services, manufacturing, or social businesses. You will be able to design your consulting framework to address the unique issues and opportunities presented by your target market if you have a thorough understanding of the pain points, needs, and preferences of that market.

3. **Defining Your Consulting Services**: It is important to provide a detailed description of the consulting services that you will be providing in India. Determine how your expertise may provide value to the customers you are trying to reach, whether it be through the provision of market research, the development of strategy, the optimization of processes, or any other area in which you have specialized knowledge. Create a distinctive selling concept that will set your consulting business apart from that of your rivals

4. **Developing a Methodology:** The first stage in developing a methodology is to develop a step-by-step methodology that specifies the consulting process from beginning to end. This should entail gathering data, identifying objectives,

67

conducting early assessments, analyzing findings, generating suggestions, and putting solutions into action. Modify this process so that it meets the specific criteria of the industry and market that you are targeting.

5. **Leveraging Technology and Innovation:** If you want to stay ahead of the competition in the ever-changing Indian business environment, include technology and innovation into your consulting strategy. Make use of various digital tools for data analysis, managing projects, and communicating with others. Investigate new developments in areas such as artificial intelligence, blockchain technology, and environmentally responsible business practices so that you may provide your customers with innovative solutions.

6. **Continuous Learning and Improvement:** A productive consulting framework is not static but rather develops over the course of time. Maintain a current awareness of the most recent developments, best practices, and regulatory shifts in your business. Maintain a steady stream of communication with your customers to get feedback, monitor your progress, and adjust your approach, as necessary. In order to increase the value that you offer to your customers, you should embrace a culture of continual learning and improvement.

You will be in an advantageous position to manage the intricacies of beginning a business in India if you build a solid consulting structure and methodology. It does not matter if you are launching a social enterprise, a manufacturing firm, a consultancy business, or a technology startup; the principles stated in this subchapter will serve as your roadmap to success no matter what kind of business you are launching. Always keep in mind that your consulting company's development and long-term viability will be directly correlated to its capacity to innovate, adapt, and demonstrate an in-depth understanding of the Indian market.

Promotional Activities and the Acquiring of Customers in India

When it comes to the success of a new business venture in India, one of the most crucial factors is how successfully the company markets itself and recruits new customers. Because the Indian market is so large and varied, it presents a wealth of chances to ambitious business owners in a variety of fields, including sustainable businesses, tech startups, consulting organizations, manufacturing businesses, and social enterprises. Nevertheless, successfully navigating this intricate market calls for an approach that is intelligent and purposeful.

To begin, it is vital to have a good understanding of the Indian consumer. India is a country that is home to a wide variety of ethnic groups, linguistic groups, and socioeconomic backgrounds. Because of this, it is absolutely necessary to carry out in-depth market research in order to determine who your target audience is and adapt your marketing efforts accordingly. It does not matter if you are trying to acquire customers for a digital startup that is aimed at urban millennials or for a social venture that is aimed at rural communities; having a solid understanding of their requirements, preferences, and purchasing patterns will be essential.

Building relationships and gaining one another's trust are extremely important aspects of conducting business in India. Events for networking, conferences in one's sector, and trade exhibitions are all wonderful opportunities to meet with possible customers, partners, and authorities in one's field. Participating in these events can assist you in establishing your credibility and expanding your professional network, both of which can be extremely useful when it comes to getting new clients.

Utilizing digital media is another essential component of successful marketing in India. Digital marketing has developed into an effective method that can be used to communicate with a large number of people as a direct result of the rapid expansion of Internet use, social media, and online shopping. You may greatly increase your exposure and attract potential customers by developing a robust online presence. This can be accomplished by developing a website with a superior design, optimizing your website for search engines, and running engaging social media campaigns.

In addition, word-of-mouth marketing has a significant amount of weight in India. Your company's reputation can be dramatically impacted by happy consumers and positive reviews, which can in turn help you bring in new customers. As a result, it is of the utmost importance to provide excellent service to customers and to provide goods and services of the highest possible quality.

Last but not least, it is essential to have a solid awareness of the local legislation and regulatory standards that are associated with marketing in India. You will be able to avoid legal issues and develop confidence among your customers if you ensure compliance with advertising standards, data protection laws, and consumer protection legislation.

In conclusion, marketing in India and attracting customers there calls for a multifaceted strategy that considers the country's broad consumer base, the significance of cultivating connections, making effective use of digital channels, and providing outstanding customer service. Aspiring business owners in India can efficiently reach their target audience and launch a profitable enterprise by first gaining a grasp of the local market, then customizing their marketing efforts, and finally ensuring that they remain in compliance with all applicable legislation.

Increasing Your Clientele and Developing Your Consulting Practice

If you are interested in beginning your own business in India, one lucrative option is to go into the consulting industry. Consulting services are in high demand across a variety of company sectors, and if you employ the appropriate tactics, you will be able to successfully build and expand your consulting business in this expansive and varied market.

1. **Find your sweet spot:** It is essential, before expanding your consulting business, to zero down on your specific area of expertise. Determine the particular sector or field in which you have expertise and where you can add value to clients' experiences. This can help you differentiate yourself from other businesses in your industry and attract the customers you want to work with.

2. **Create a robust network:** Networking is an essential component of every successful firm, but it is especially important in the consulting sector. Attending industry conferences, signing up for membership in professional organizations, and networking with prospective customers and business allies. Developing a robust network will not only assist you in acquiring new customers, but it will also create prospects for joint ventures and professional advancement.

3. **Use technology to your advantage:** In this day and age, the use of technology can be a key factor in the growth of your consulting business. Embrace the hardware and software that can improve the efficiency of your operations, speed up your workflow, and deepen your connection with your customers. For maximum effectiveness and output, make use of tools for project management, customer relationship management (CRM) software, and online collaboration platforms.

4. **Hire talented and smart people:** You will need staff to handle the rising amount of work as your consulting business expands, so it is important that you hire and train the correct talent. Employ competent people whose personal beliefs coincide with those of your company and who have the required abilities and levels of experience. Make an investment in their training and development to guarantee that they will be able to provide impressive results to customers.

71

5. **Provide a wide range of services:** If you want to grow your consulting business, you should think about expanding the range of services you offer. Determine other spheres of activity in which you may contribute value and broaden the scope of your skills. You will be able to serve a more diverse range of customers as a result, which will result in increased revenue streams.

6. **Establishing strategic relationships:** Establishing strategic relationships is important since working with other companies and people can lead to the discovery of new chances for expansion. Find possible strategic partners whose skills match your own and who can direct clients in your direction. Establishing relationships with others that are advantageous to both parties might assist you in broadening your audience and boosting your credibility.

7. **Pay attention to your clients:** Pay attention to the level of pleasure experienced by your clients, as this will increase the likelihood that they will recommend your services to others, so aiding in the expansion of your consulting business. Putting the needs of the client first means consistently producing high-quality work, going above and beyond their expectations, and offering outstanding customer service. Maintain close vigilance over the comments and ideas made by customers, and always aim for the highest possible level of performance.

In order to scale and build your consulting firm in India, you will require meticulous preparation, the ability to make smart decisions, and an approach that is customer centric. You can achieve sustainable growth and establish your consulting business as a reputable and sought-after service provider in the market if you capitalize on your experience, build a strong network, embrace technology, and focus on client happiness. These are the four pillars on which sustainable growth is built.

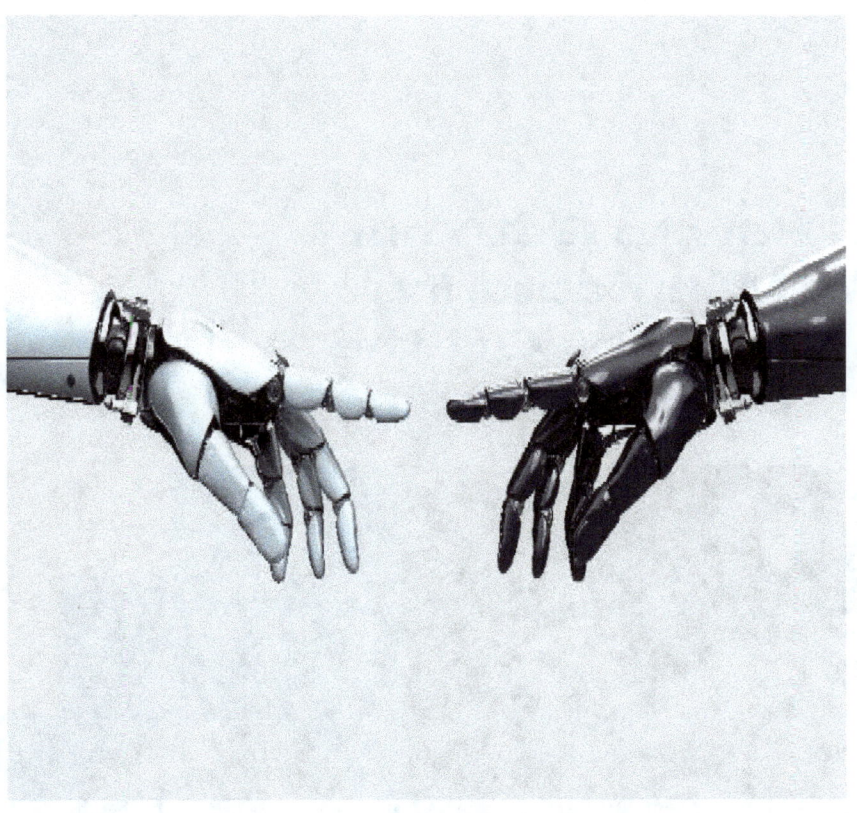

How to Get Your Manufacturing Company Off the Ground in India

CHAPTER-6

CHAPTER 6: HOW TO GET YOUR MANUFACTURING COMPANY OFF THE GROUND IN INDIA

An Exposition on the Manufacturing Industry in India

The manufacturing industry in India has quickly established itself as an important contributor to the expansion and growth of the country's economy. It has become a desirable location for prospective business owners who are interested in beginning their ventures in India due to the immense potential it possesses and the variety of options it presents. In this subchapter, we will present you with an overview of the manufacturing industry in India and explore the potential, obstacles, and critical factors that are involved in launching a manufacturing business in India.

The manufacturing sector in India has seen tremendous growth throughout the years, contributing to the Gross Domestic Product as well as the generation of employment opportunities. The sector comprises a wide variety of industries, such as the automotive industry, textile manufacturing, chemical manufacturing, pharmaceutical manufacturing, electronic manufacturing, and machinery manufacturing. India presents an enormous opportunity for businesspeople who are interested in entering the manufacturing sector because the country has a vast and expanding consumer market, a competent labour, and favorable government policies.

The availability of labour that is less expensive than other options is one of the primary benefits that comes with beginning a manufacturing firm in India. Because this nation has access to such a large pool of skilled and semi-skilled labourers, it is an attractive location for businesses that rely heavily on human labour. In addition, the government of India has launched a number of campaigns to promote manufacturing, such as the "Make in India" campaign. This campaign has two primary goals: to increase production within India and to entice investment from outside the country.

However, beginning a manufacturing business in India is not without its share of obstacles to overcome. Entrepreneurs may face challenges in the form of inadequate infrastructure, cumbersome bureaucratic procedures, and overly complex regulatory frameworks. As a result, it is absolutely necessary to conduct extensive research on and get a solid grasp of the legal and regulatory standards that are unique to the manufacturing industry.

Aspiring business owners in India need to consider a number of important aspects before launching a manufacturing enterprise. Researching the market and choosing the appropriate product or market niche are two key factors that will determine how successful the company will be. Entrepreneurs can make informed judgments if they have a solid understanding of the dynamics of demand and supply, as well as the target market and the competition in that market.

In addition, maintaining a competitive edge in the manufacturing industry requires making effective use of modern technologies and innovative ideas. Explore prospects in renewable energy, clean technology, and smart manufacturing solutions if you are an aspiring entrepreneur in India looking to launch a tech startup or a sustainable business.

In summing up, the manufacturing industry in India offers an enormous amount of opportunity for ambitious business owners in a variety of fields, such as those interested in starting software startups, sustainable businesses, consulting organizations, or social enterprises. Entrepreneurs in India may turn their ideas for successful manufacturing businesses into reality by first gaining a grasp of the dynamics of the market, then capitalizing on innovation, and then navigating the regulatory framework.

Opportunities for Manufacturing in India, Studied and Identified

The manufacturing sector in India is seeing substantial growth, which is giving an abundance of options for budding business owners. India has become a mecca for companies seeking to build manufacturing operations as a result of the country's fast-growing consumer market, its highly skilled labour, and the steps taken by the Indian government to promote manufacturing. This subchapter's goal is to assist ambitious business owners in recognizing and making the most of the opportunities available in the manufacturing sector in India.

Beginning a manufacturing enterprise in India may prove to be a fruitful endeavor, particularly in industries such as textiles, chemicals, automotive, electronics, and renewable energy. Manufacturing companies benefit from the country's large population of potential customers, as well as the supportive policies of the nation's government and the wealth of natural resources.

Conducting in-depth market research is one of the first steps in the process of locating potential manufacturing possibilities. In order to find possible niches, business owners should do an analysis of current trends, demand patterns, and market gaps. Entrepreneurs can detect holes in the market and produce creative items that meet consumer expectations if they gain an awareness of the wants and needs of Indian consumers as well as their preferences.

In addition, would-be business owners had to take into consideration the technical climate in India. As a result of the country's exceptional technological progress, it has become an excellent location for the establishment of innovative technology businesses. The use of technology in production procedures can improve efficiency, which in turn leads to lower costs and higher levels of output. Businesses in the manufacturing sector can gain a competitive advantage in the Indian market by investigating emerging technologies such as automation, robots, and artificial intelligence (AI).

When searching for chances for manufacturing in India,

sustainability is an additional factor that is essential to take into consideration. There is a rising demand for items that are both sustainable and environmentally friendly as people become more conscious of environmental issues. This market segment can be penetrated by business owners who embrace environmentally friendly production practices, make use of renewable energy sources, and place an emphasis on recycling and waste reduction.

Additionally, ambitious business owners can investigate the possibility of working in the manufacturing industry by providing consultancy services. The manufacturing sector in India requires specialists with knowledge and experience in a variety of fields, such as supply chain management, quality control, and regulatory compliance. Entrepreneurs can distinguish themselves as authorities in their field by establishing themselves as consultants in the industrial sector by giving their services to already established companies.

In conclusion, social enterprises have quickly become extremely well-known in India. Entrepreneurs have the ability to make a beneficial impact on society while also producing money if they combine their business aims and their impact on the community. Manufacturing companies can look for ways to help local communities, promote fair trade practices, or support marginalized groups by exploring the opportunities available to them.

In summing up, those who are interested in starting their own businesses will find an abundance of prospects in India's manufacturing industry. Entrepreneurs in India can identify and exploit possibilities in the manufacturing sector by undertaking market research, adopting technology, concentrating on sustainability, investigating consulting services, and taking into consideration the influence of their business on society. Entrepreneurs in India may transform their ideas for successful manufacturing businesses into profitable enterprises if they have the correct business plan and a comprehensive understanding of the Indian market.

Establishing a Manufacturing Establishment in India

The fact that India has become a global manufacturing powerhouse has opened up a vast number of doors for businesspeople who are interested in beginning their own manufacturing operations. India offers a favourable environment for the establishment of manufacturing companies thanks to the country's sizable population of potential customers, highly educated labour force, and business-friendly regulations at the national level. This subchapter will walk aspiring business owners through the steps involved in establishing a manufacturing unit in India. It will cover crucial topics such as the selection of a location, the fulfillment of legal criteria, the availability of financing choices, and the provision of government incentives.

When establishing a manufacturing unit, it is absolutely necessary to select an appropriate location. It is important to take into account a variety of aspects, including the availability of trained labour, closeness to raw resources, infrastructure for transportation, and access to markets. Industrial corridors and Special Economic Zones (also known as SEZs) are popular options because of the infrastructure amenities and tax advantages that they offer. In order to determine the most appropriate site, conducting an in-depth market analysis and gaining an insight into the target population can be of great assistance.

Once they have decided where to set up shop, entrepreneurs are responsible for meeting all of the necessary legal criteria. This requires the acquisition of the appropriate licenses and permissions, such as the Factory License, the Environmental Clearance, and the Industrial License. It is vital to have a solid understanding of labour laws, taxation regulations, and the rights associated with intellectual property in order to ensure smooth operations and avoid legal difficulties.

It can be difficult to secure financing for a manufacturing unit, but there are a few different possibilities to consider. Entrepreneurs have the option of investigating programmes offered by the government, venture capital funds, and bank loans that have been developed expressly for the manufacturing sector. When it comes to securing the necessary money and making the most of available financial resources, working together with financial institutions and consulting with financial experts can be helpful.

In order to encourage domestic production, the government of India has established a number of programmes and financial incentives. Under initiatives such as Make in India and Startup India, prospective business owners have the opportunity to qualify for financial aid in the form of tax breaks, subsidies, and grants. Understanding these programmes and the requirements necessary to participate in them can provide business owners with a competitive advantage and help them make the most of their profits.

In addition, establishing a manufacturing facility in India calls for efficient management of the supply chain, quality control procedures, and the adoption of environmentally responsible business practices. The efficiency of production, the amount of trash generated, and the incorporation of environmentally friendly technologies should be the primary focuses of entrepreneurs. Productivity and competitiveness can both be improved by embracing the ideas of Industry 4.0, which include automation and digitization.

In conclusion, establishing a manufacturing unit in India presents potential business owners with an enormous number of chances. An entrepreneur in India can successfully launch a manufacturing company by giving careful consideration to the location of the firm, adhering to the legal requirements, acquiring funding, and making use of the incentives provided by the Indian government. To ensure prosperity over the long term and to contribute to the economic growth of the country, it is important to place an emphasis on environmentally responsible practices and to utilize the most advanced technologies.

Taking Charge of Logistics and Supply Chain Management in India

The effective management of a company's supply chain and logistics in today's interconnected global economy is essential to that company's financial and operational success. Aspiring business owners in India can benefit from the information contained in this subchapter, which will instruct them on how to efficiently manage their supply chain and logistics operations. If you are establishing a tech startup, a sustainable business, a consultancy firm, a manufacturing venture, or a social enterprise, understanding and following best practices in supply chain management will greatly contribute to the success and sustainability of your organization. This is the case regardless of the type of business you are beginning.

Acquiring a Solid Understanding of the Indian Market: The rapidly expanding economy of India presents countless chances for business owners. Having said that, it does in fact create certain one-of-a-kind difficulties in terms of supply chain and logistics. To successfully navigate the Indian market, one needs to take a well-planned and flexible approach due to the country's enormous geographical spread, unique cultural backdrop, and varying levels of infrastructure development.

Important Things to Keep in Mind:

1. **Infrastructure:** Determine the extent of the available infrastructure in the areas where you intend to conduct business. Determine where possible bottlenecks could occur, and then design alternative travel paths or forms of transportation in response.

2. **Networking:** Establishing solid ties with local vendors, suppliers, and logistics partners is an absolutely necessary step in the process of developing local partnerships. They have vital insights into the dynamics of the local market

and can assist you in streamlining the operations of your supply chain.

3. **Regulatory Compliance:** Be sure you are familiar with the intricate regulatory structure that governs the supply chain and logistics in India in order to ensure regulatory compliance. Make sure that you are in compliance with all of the legal obligations, such as those pertaining to permits, licenses, and taxes.

4. **Adopting New Technologies:** If you want your supply chain operations to run more efficiently, you should embrace innovative technologies. Utilize cloud-based inventory management systems, adopt GPS tracking for real-time shipment monitoring, and use data analytics to enhance your ability to make sound judgments.

5. **Last-Mile Delivery:** Create effective techniques for providing last-mile delivery in order to meet the needs of India's varied client base. Utilize the knowledge of the locals in order to overcome obstacles such as traffic congestion, being in a rural place, and having limited infrastructure.

6. **Green Supply Chain:** Incorporating environmentally friendly business practices into your supply chain is critical if you wish to remain competitive in the Indian market as the importance of sustainability continues to rise. Investigate several possibilities, such as environmentally friendly packaging, ethical sourcing, and renewable energy sources, in order to entice conscientious customers.

In order to effectively manage the supply chain and logistics in India, one must have a full awareness of the market's distinctive qualities and the difficulties it presents. Aspiring business owners may create a supply chain system that is solid and effective by investing in infrastructure, cultivating local alliances, ensuring regulatory compliance, utilizing technology, optimizing last-mile deliveries, and embracing sustainability. Not only will your company's operational efficiency improve thanks to your successful management of the supply chain and logistics, but it will also help the overall growth and success of your company in the Indian market.

Maintaining Quality and Expanding the Scope of Your Manufacturing Company

In the fast-paced and cutthroat environment of the manufacturing industry, quality control is absolutely essential to the survival and expansion of any company. Aspiring business owners in India who are interested in beginning a manufacturing enterprise need to have a solid understanding of the significance of upholding high-quality standards and how to scale their operations in an efficient manner.

Establishing quality standards that are both specific and comprehensive for your products is one of the first things you should do to ensure quality control. In order to accomplish this, particular criteria need to be established about the materials, size, usefulness, and performance. These standards serve as a reference point against which all items are evaluated, which helps to maintain consistency and ensures that customers are happy. You will be able to monitor and oversee the entire manufacturing process with the assistance of a sophisticated quality management system, which will also assist you in locating any deviations or flaws at an earlier stage.

It is absolutely necessary to make investments in dependable production equipment and technological advancements in order to meet these quality standards. The quality and precision of your products can be significantly improved by upgrading to more modern machinery and software, which not only increases productivity but also saves time. Maintaining and calibrating your equipment on a regular basis will both protect it from unforeseen faults and guarantee the output of a quality that is consistent with expectations.

In addition, one of the most important aspects of quality control is providing your workers with training and opportunities for advancement. When it comes to manufacturing high-quality goods, having staff members that are experienced and skilled is quite necessary. Provide your employees with training on the significance of quality control, covering topics such as the correct way to handle equipment and the observance of standard operating procedures. Identifying and resolving any quality concerns in a timely manner can be facilitated by encouraging open communication and feedback loops.

Scaling quickly becomes an important focus for your manufacturing company as it begins to expand its operations. Scaling refers to the process of growing your production capacity and capabilities to fulfill an ever-increasing number of customer orders. This can be accomplished through the use of a variety of tactics, such as making investments in new machinery, improving the efficiency of your manufacturing line, or contracting certain processes out to a third party. It is essential to plan meticulously in advance in order to guarantee that the quality of your products will not suffer as a result of scaling. Maintaining quality standards while simultaneously increasing output requires constant monitoring and evaluation of business processes.

Lastly, utilizing technology effectively can be a huge help when it comes to quality control and scaling. You may gain real-time insights into your manufacturing processes by implementing automation and data analytics. This will enable you to discover bottlenecks, optimize workflows, and make decisions based on the data collected. Adopting digital solutions can help operations become more streamlined, reduce the number of errors made, and enhance overall efficiency.

In conclusion, a successful manufacturing business requires quality control and scale as vital components. Aspiring business owners in India may assure consistent quality and effectively scale their manufacturing operations by establishing defined quality standards, investing in the appropriate equipment, training their workers, and leveraging technology. Always keep in mind that quality is not only an endpoint but rather an ongoing journey towards perfection.

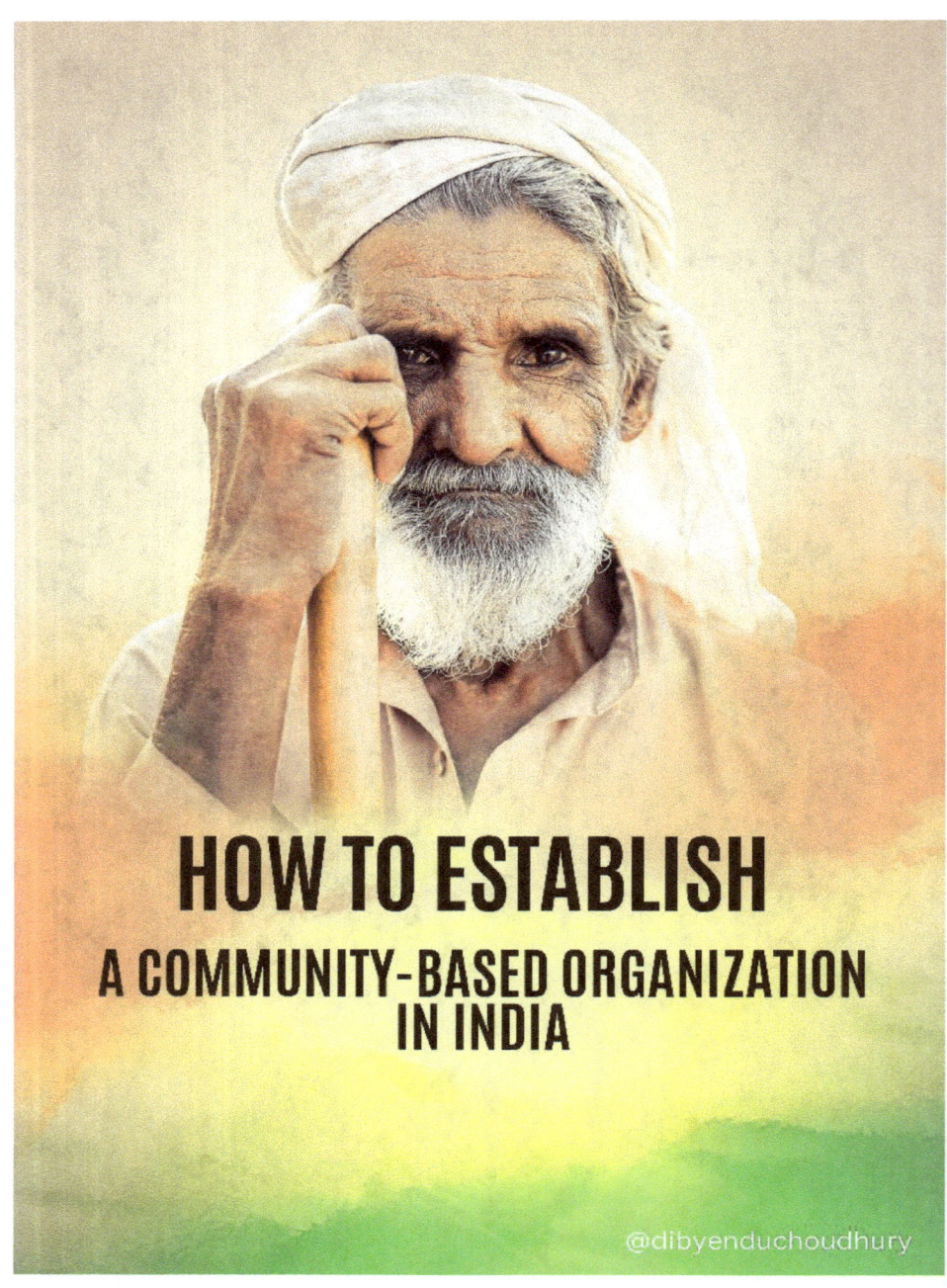

HOW TO ESTABLISH
A COMMUNITY-BASED ORGANIZATION IN INDIA

@dibyenduchoudhury

CHAPTER 7: HOW TO ESTABLISH A COMMUNITY-BASED ORGANIZATION IN INDIA

Gaining an Understanding of the Social Entrepreneurship Scene in India

In recent years, India has seen an increase in the number of social companies, which has been driven by a growing awareness of the country's social and environmental problems. These companies, which are also known as impact-driven firms, have the dual objectives of making a profit and making a positive and lasting social impact. Understanding the ecosystem of social entrepreneurship in India is essential if you want to launch a company in the country with a mission that goes beyond producing a profit for its owners.

The social enterprise sector in India is extremely broad and vibrant, spanning a wide variety of business fields and industry categories. Social companies are solving a wide range of important social and environmental concerns, ranging from education and healthcare to renewable energy and agriculture. Typically, what sets these businesses apart from others in their industry is the unique nature of their business models, which strike a healthy balance between financial viability and positive social effect.

The favourable regulatory environment in India is one of the primary reasons that is contributing to the growth of social enterprises in the country. The government of India has established a number of different policies and programmes in order to encourage and facilitate the practice of social entrepreneurship. For example, the Companies Act of 2013 ushered in the notion of a "Socially Responsible Business" and mandated that eligible businesses spend a specific percentage of their revenues on corporate social responsibility (CSR) initiatives. This legislation was intended to encourage more charitable and environmentally conscious business practices. Because of this, a growing number of companies are embracing the concept of social enterprise.

In addition, a number of incubators, accelerators, and impact investment funds have recently sprouted up in India in order to provide support for social entrepreneurs. Mentoring, financial support, and opportunities to make connections are provided by these organizations, all of which are vital to the success of a business. In addition to this, they provide entrepreneurs with specialized programmes and tools to assist them in navigating the one-of-a-kind obstacles that are presented by social companies.

In order to launch a successful social company in India, you will need to zero in on a serious social or environmental problem that is in line with your interests and capabilities. Carry out in-depth research to acquire an understanding of the intended beneficiaries, the solutions that are currently available, and the possible market prospects. It is of equal importance to have a strong business strategy that strikes a balance between financial viability and positive social effect.

In the world of social entrepreneurship, networking and teamwork are two of the most important skills to have. Engage in conversation with other business owners in a similar position, as well as experts in your field and possible business allies, to both expand your horizons and your circle of support. Your social venture may be more successful if you work with other organizations, such as non-governmental organizations (NGOs), government agencies, and local communities.

In general, beginning a social enterprise in India presents a multitude of options to make a significant contribution to the improvement of society. Aspiring business owners can embark on a path that combines financial success with social impact and contributes to the nation's sustainable development goals by first gaining a grasp of the social enterprise landscape and then maximizing the use of the resources that are at their disposal.

Finding Out What the Social Problems and Impact Areas Are in India

As aspiring businesspeople in India, it is essential for you to be aware of the social problems and impact areas that currently exist inside the nation. You may establish enterprises that not only make profits but also contribute to the improvement of society if you have an awareness of these obstacles and how to overcome them. In this subchapter, we will discuss how you can create a business that addresses the numerous social issues that are widespread in India, as well as analyze the various social challenges that are present in India.

India is a varied nation that faces a wide variety of societal challenges, including but not limited to poverty, illiteracy, access to healthcare, gender inequity, environmental degradation, and many more. Each of these problems carries with it a one-of-a-kind opportunity for company owners to make a positive difference while simultaneously developing profitable enterprises.

If you are an aspiring entrepreneur in India looking to launch a tech firm, you might want to consider concentrating your efforts on developing solutions that close the digital gap. The overwhelming majority of people in India are not connected to the Internet or have access to modern technology. You can make a positive social impact while also tapping into a market that has the potential to be lucrative if you build cutting-edge technology solutions that are tailored to meet the requirements of these underserved populations.

There is a growing demand for environmentally friendly goods and services, which is good news for entrepreneurs interested in beginning a sustainable business in India. Not only will addressing environmental issues such as air and water pollution, waste management, and renewable energy contribute to India being a cleaner and healthier country, but it will also attract customers who are concerned about the environment.

Businesses providing consulting services have the potential to make major contributions toward the resolution of societal problems in India. It is possible for you to make a contribution to the overall growth of the country if you work in fields such as education, healthcare, and social welfare and provide organizations and individuals working in such fields with expert advice and direction.

Entrepreneurs who are interested in the manufacturing industry may choose to concentrate on either the creation of job opportunities for underserved communities or the production of items that are both affordable and of high quality for people with lower incomes. You can contribute to the eradication of poverty and the social empowerment of others by adopting inclusive and ethical business practices into your manufacturing company.

Lastly, if you want to make a profit while also having a positive impact on the community, launching a social company in India is the way to go. Social businesses have the ability to bring about a revolutionary change in the lives of many people, whether it is through the provision of solutions to the problem of dirty water, the empowerment of rural craftsmen, or the improvement of access to healthcare in remote places.

As a conclusion, it is essential for ambitious business owners to investigate the social problems and impact areas that exist in India. If you are able to gain an awareness of the specific difficulties that are faced by society, you will be able to establish enterprises that will not only be successful but will also contribute to the improvement of the country. In India, there are an abundance of options to create a positive effect while also developing a successful business, regardless of whether you are starting a software startup, a sustainable business, a consulting firm, a manufacturing operation, or a social enterprise.

Developing a Model for Socially Responsible Business in India
Entrepreneurs who want to use their companies to make the world a better place would find India to be an ideal environment thanks

to the country's diversified population and its own set of distinct socioeconomic difficulties. The idea of a social business model has been gaining major support in the country over the past few years, as an increasing number of business owners become aware of the possibility of combining financial gain with the achievement of social goals. This subchapter examines the essential components of developing a social business model in India. It is written for aspiring business owners who are enthusiastic about the prospect of launching a company that can bring about transformational change in the world.

To get started, it is essential to have a fundamental understanding of what constitutes a social business model. A social business, in contrast to conventional companies whose main objective is to maximize profits, seeks to solve a social problem while simultaneously building a steady customer base and revenue stream. Through the utilization of this one-of-a-kind strategy, business owners are afforded the opportunity to combat urgent issues such as widespread poverty, inadequate educational opportunities, inadequate medical care, and unsustainable environmental practices, all while assuring the continued success of their respective enterprises.

When beginning a social enterprise in India, it is vital to determine the specific problem that the enterprise will work to solve in the market. In this regard, it is essential to carry out extensive market research and have a solid understanding of the particular requirements of the target demographic. An entrepreneur who is interested in enhancing education in rural areas, for instance, can investigate novel approaches to the problem, such as interactive learning platforms, tablets available at a low cost, or programmes that train teachers.

Finding the optimal equilibrium between a company's social effect and its ability to be financially viable is another essential component of developing a social business model in India. It is possible that the primary goal is to bring about positive change; nonetheless, earning steady money is absolutely necessary to ensure the life of the organization. This can be accomplished through a variety of revenue streams, such as the sale of products or services, the receipt of grants or donations, or the formation of partnerships with governmental or charitable organizations.

In order for a social enterprise to be successful in India, collaboration and partnership are two crucial components that must be present. Engaging with organizations that have the same mission as one's own, whether they are in the public or private sector, can provide access to resources, knowledge, and a wider network, so increasing the influence and reach of the business. In addition, fostering a sense of ownership and ensuring the project's continued viability can be accomplished through forming partnerships with local communities and incorporating them into the decision-making process.

Last but not least, budding social entrepreneurs in India have the additional challenge of navigating the legal and regulatory landscape that is unique to their particular field. It is absolutely necessary for compliance and smooth operation to have a solid understanding of the legal requirements, the tax implications, and the appropriate rules. Entrepreneurs that actively participate in industry associations, seek the counsel of qualified experts, and keep abreast of the most recent advancements in their sector can efficiently navigate the complicated terrain that they face.

To summarize, developing a social business model in India necessitates having an in-depth knowledge of the societal problems that need to be addressed, a dedication to the development of sustainable revenue, collaboration with a wide variety of stakeholders, and adherence to the numerous legal and regulatory frameworks. Aspiring business owners can embark on the road to launching a company that not only achieves commercial success but also has a beneficial and long-lasting effect on the community if they take these factors into consideration and include them in their plans.

Fundraising Efforts and Financial Support for Non-Profit Organizations

Aspiring business owners in India need to be aware that launching a social company involves not just a fantastic idea and an ardent desire to have a beneficial impact, but also sufficient financial backing in order to get off the ground. In this subchapter, we will discuss a variety of approaches to fundraising and finance that you might utilize in order to bring your idea for a social enterprise closer to being a reality.

1. **Bootstrapping**: Using your own personal money or resources to fund your endeavor is one of the most frequent ways to establish a social enterprise. Bootstrapping is one of the most common strategies to start a social enterprise. This approach enables you to keep complete control over your business, but it may restrict the amount of space available for expansion.

2. **Grants and Other Forms of Financial Assistance**: The government of India provides a number of financial assistance programmes and grants to organizations that are working to improve society and ensure its continued existence. These awards may be awarded by governmental agencies, private foundations, or organizations that work only for charitable purposes. It is necessary to conduct study, locate the appropriate funding, and support systems that are open to your particular type of social enterprise niche. In India Bootstrapping to start-up and later finding the Govt. or other funding works much better and viable business model.

3. **Effect Investors:** An individual or organization that invests in social enterprises with the goal of generating both financial returns and verifiable social or environmental effects is known as an impact investor. In recent years, India has seen a substantial rise in the popularity of impact investing, with the country becoming home to a number of funds and networks devoted to the support of social

entrepreneurs.

4. **Crowdfunding:** Crowdfunding has quickly become one of the most common ways for nonprofit organizations to acquire much-needed financial resources. You can solicit individual contributions from people who are interested in your cause by publicizing your proposal and the potential impact it could have on a larger audience. Crowdfunding not only offers money assistance, but it also assists in the formation of a community of individuals who support your cause.

5. **Capital de risqué social:** Your social enterprise will be able to fulfil its impact goals and scale with the assistance of these companies, which give finance and guidance. Establishing connections with firms that provide social venture capital can provide the essential help and knowledge to handle the hurdles of beginning a social enterprise.

6. **Building strategic collaborations and partnerships:** Building strategic collaborations and partnerships with other organizations that have a similar mission can be an effective way to use the resources, networks, and skills of those other organizations. This strategy not only brings in new financing but also boosts the legitimacy of your social organization and expands its potential customer base.

Remember, fundraising for ethical enterprises demands a special approach. Potential investors and funders are interested not just in the financial returns your business may provide, but also in the impact it can have. As a result, it is of the utmost importance to design an enticing and well described business strategy that is capable of conveying both the potential for your organization's financial viability and its social impact.

To summarize, India is a suitable place to launch a social company; the most important steps to take are to raise money and get finance. Aspiring business owners can gain the required resources to transform their idea for a social enterprise into a reality while also making a meaningful influence on society by investigating a variety of funding possibilities such as self-funding, grants, impact investors, crowdfunding, social venture capital, and collaborations.

Assessing the Positive and Negative Effects That Your Business Has on Society

In today's world, where it is increasingly expected of businesses to contribute to society and have a positive influence, it has become vital to measure and evaluate the social impact of your firm. Not only will knowing how to effectively assess and evaluate your social impact as a prospective entrepreneur in India help you attract investors and consumers, but it will also help you promote genuine change in your community.

1. **Determining What Social Impact:** Means It is essential before you can measure and analyze your social impact, to first determine what social impact means for your particular business. Are you more concerned with the long-term health of the environment, the reduction of poverty, or education? To ensure that your impact-measuring initiatives are successful, clearly describe your social objective.

2. **Defining Essential Metrics**: Once you have established your social mission, the next step is to determine the essential metrics that are in line with your objectives. If your company's mission is to alleviate poverty, for instance, one metric you could track is the number of people who have been raised over the poverty line; another would be an increase in the average income; still, another would be access to essential goods.

3. **Data Both Quantitative and Qualitative:** You need a combination of quantitative and qualitative data in order to accurately quantify the impact that an organization has on

society. Quantitative data might contain things like figures and statistics, such as the quantity of waste reduced or the number of people who benefited from the programme. The collection of tales, anecdotes, and feedback from stakeholders is an example of qualitative data. The goal of this type of data is to gain an understanding of the qualitative changes that have been brought about by your business.

4. **Establishing a Baseline and Evaluating**: Its influence First and foremost, you should establish a baseline against which to evaluate its influence. You will be able to demonstrate the efficacy of your projects and monitor their progress with the help of this. Conduct impact assessments on a regular basis in order to analyze the improvements that your company has made and to locate areas in which it may improve.

5. **Participation of Stakeholders:** Participate in dialogue with your stakeholders, which may include beneficiaries, investors, employees, and members of the community, in order to collect their points of view and comments. Their contributions can give you invaluable insights into the efficiency of the social impact activities you are undertaking.

6. **Reporting and Communication:** Be as open and honest as possible with your stakeholders when communicating the outcomes of your social impact measurements and evaluations. Think about compiling an impact report that details your accomplishments, the obstacles you have overcome, and your long-term objectives. Make use of this research to entice investors, stimulate interest among customers, and establish credibility for your business.

Keep in mind that calculating and assessing the extent of your social influence is an ongoing effort. Reviewing and improving your measurements and methods on a consistent basis will guarantee that they are accurate and relevant. You may not only be a force for positive change but also differentiate your business in the cutthroat Indian market if you understand and accurately measure your social impact.

This section is helpful for ambitious business owners who are interested in beginning their venture in India, regardless of the sector in which they plan to operate. Understanding how to assess and analyze your social impact is essential to your success in today's socially conscious marketplace, regardless of whether you want to launch a social enterprise, a digital startup, a sustainable business, a consultancy business, a manufacturing firm, or any of the aforementioned types of businesses.

Chapter-8

CONCLUDING REMARKS AND MOVING FORWARD

@DIBYENDUCHOUDHURY

CHAPTER 8: CONCLUDING REMARKS AND MOVING FORWARD

A Recap of the Most Important Takeaways

You should be congratulated, ambitious company owners, on having finished reading our detailed guide to beginning a business in India. We have covered a wide variety of topics throughout this book, "From Idea to Reality: A Guide to Starting a Business in India," including how to create a software startup, a sustainable business, a consulting firm, a manufacturing business, and a social enterprise in India. Now that we have covered all of these different niches, let us go back over some of the most important things we learned.

How to Get Your Business Off the Ground in India:

1. The first step in understanding the Indian market is to carry out extensive research and analysis in order to uncover market potential, cultural subtleties, and consumer preferences. Legal and regulatory requirements:

2. Become familiar with the licenses, permissions, and registrations that are required in order to create and run a business in India.

3. Options for financing: Investigate a variety of funding sources, including bank loans, venture capital, angel investors, and programmes offered by the government, in order to get the required funds.

4. 4. Building a solid network requires establishing connections with other business owners, industry professionals, and mentors at networking events, conferences, and online groups in order to obtain new perspectives and receive assistance.

How to Get Your Tech Startup Off the Ground in India:

1. Embrace the digital transformation: Develop creative technological solutions by capitalizing on India's expanding digital infrastructure and the country's high smartphone penetration rate.
2. Acquiring talent requires that you offer competitive compensation, provide a favorable working environment, and cultivate a culture of innovation in order to attract and keep the top technical talent in your industry.
3. Protection of intellectual property: Be sure to protect your ideas, patents, copyrights, and trademarks so that you can have an advantage over your competitors in the fast-paced technology market.
4. Start-up accelerators and incubators are programmes that you should seriously consider enrolling in if you want to obtain access to funding, mentoring, and networking possibilities that are unique to the technology industry.

How to Establish a Profitable and Long-Lasting Business in India:

1. Focus on the environmental and social effects of your business: incorporate sustainable practices into your business model to solve major concerns such as climate change, resource depletion, and social injustice.
2. Collaborate with organizations that share your values: Seek relationships with non-governmental organizations (NGOs), government entities, and businesses that are focused on sustainability to magnify your influence and reach a wider audience.
3. Green certifications and standards: In order to improve your reputation and show that you are committed to sustainability, you should obtain relevant certifications such as LEED, GRI, or ISO.
4. Circular economy and waste management: Investigate novel approaches to reduce the amount of waste produced, encourage recycling, and implement a circular strategy for the

management of resources.

How to Launch a Successful Consulting Practice in India:

1. Establish your area of expertise by identifying your market niche and working to establish a set of specialized skills that differentiates you from other rivals.
2. Establish contacts with potential clients, industry leaders, and subject matter experts in order to gain credibility and create leads while building a strong professional network.
3. Provide clients with complete solutions, personalized counsel, and strategic insights in order to develop long-term connections as part of your value-added service offering.
4. Continual education and professional development include keeping abreast of developments in your sector, participating in relevant conferences, and pursuing relevant certifications in order to improve your consulting abilities.

How to Get Your Manufacturing Company Off the Ground in India:

1. Gain an understanding of the landscape of the manufacturing industry by conducting research into the needs of the present market, the logistics of the supply chain, and the capabilities of the manufacturing facility.
2. Infrastructure and logistics: evaluate the availability of the necessary utilities, transportation, and storage space for industrial processes to run smoothly.
3. Compliance and quality standards: In order to guarantee the dependability and safety of your goods, be sure to adhere to the regulatory requirements and quality certifications in place.
4. Adoption of technology and automation: Embrace cutting-edge manufacturing technologies and automation in order to improve the effectiveness of production processes and optimize production overall.

Step-by-Step Guide to Establishing a Social Enterprise in India

1. Define your social mission by clearly articulating the social or environmental problem that you intend to tackle and then aligning your company strategy accordingly.
2. Impact measurement and reporting: Create reliable metrics to quantify your organization's social impact and effectively communicate this information to stakeholders and potential investors.
3. Collaborate with communities: Involve local communities, non-governmental organizations (NGOs), and government organizations in the process of co-creating sustainable solutions to ensure the continued success of your social enterprise over the long term.
4. Funding and sustainable revenue models: Investigate the different funding possibilities available to you, such as impact investors, grants, and crowdfunding, in order to promote your social objective while also preserving your organization's financial viability.

It is important to keep in mind that beginning a business in India demands you to be dedicated, persistent, and adaptable. You will be in a better position to negotiate the obstacles that lie ahead and embrace the chances that are presented to you if you apply the major insights from this book to your particular field of expertise. Good luck with your entrepreneurial adventure!

Establishing Objectives and a Course of Action for the Beginning of Your Business in India

As an ambitious entrepreneur in India, launching your own firm can seem like a daunting endeavor. You may, however, make a successful reality out of your idea if you set the appropriate goals and have a well-thought-out plan in place. Regardless of the specific field or sector in which you aim to launch your company in India, this subchapter will walk you through the steps of formulating objectives and developing a strategy for moving forward.

It is necessary to get a fundamental comprehension of the relevance of goal setting before delving into the particulars. Setting specific goals for yourself not only helps you keep focused, but they also serve as a baseline against which you can evaluate how far you have come. The process of creating goals is the same whether you want to launch a social enterprise, a manufacturing company, a consulting firm, or a technology startup. It also does not matter what kind of business you want to launch.

Establishing what you want to accomplish with your company is the first step. What are some goals that you wish to accomplish with your company? Is it to find a solution to a problem, provide a product or service that no one else does, or have a positive effect on society? You will be able to establish a powerful vision for your company if you first define your objectives very specifically.

Following that, turn each of your goals into a series of attainable stages. At this point, your action plan should begin to take effect. Determine the activities and checkpoints that need to be reached in order for you to realize your objectives. Establish a timeline, and then distribute the available resources in accordance with it. Think about things like finance, staffing, conducting market research, meeting regulatory obligations, and producing marketing plans. Having an action plan that has been carefully considered can help you stay organized and on the right path.

In addition to this, it is vital to carry out extensive research on the Indian market as well as the nature of the competition there. It is important that you have a solid understanding of the legal and regulatory framework that applies to your business and expertise. You will be better able to recognize potential obstacles and possibilities with the use of this knowledge, which in turn will enable you to make decisions based on accurate information.

Building a strong network and finding a mentor are also essential to achieving success. Establish connections with industry professionals, entrepreneurs, and business experts who can guide and support you during your journey. These individuals will be able to assist you in achieving your goals. Joining professional communities, going to conferences, and taking part in workshops focused on a specific topic are excellent ways to broaden one's knowledge base and cultivate beneficial contacts.

In conclusion, it is important to be flexible and to be open to reevaluating both your goals and your action plan according to the circumstances. Being adaptable is essential if one is to continue to keep one step ahead in today's competitive business environment.

Keep in mind that launching a new company in India is an exciting yet difficult endeavour to undertake. You will be well on your way to successfully converting your business concept into a reality if you undertake in-depth research, create a well-defined action plan, network effectively, and maintain a flexible mindset.

Seeking Out Support and Resources for Those Looking to Start Their Own Businesses

Beginning a new business is an endeavour that is both thrilling and demanding, particularly in a nation like India. It is imperative that someone who aspires to be an entrepreneur equip themselves with the appropriate assistance and resources in order to successfully navigate the intricacies and conquer the obstacles that may come their way. In the following subsection, we will investigate a variety of different paths that may be able to offer you the required direction and aid in order to make your idea for a business a reality.

1. **Initiatives Taken by the Government:** The Indian government has taken a number of different steps to encourage startup businesses and entrepreneurial endeavors. Access to capital, tax breaks, and incubator spaces are made available to entrepreneurs through initiatives such as Make in India and Startup India. You can acquire the required financial and regulatory help to get

your firm off the ground if you make use of these resources and tap into their potential.

2. **Incubators and Accelerators:** Incubators and accelerators are several types of organizations that offer businesses a variety of resources, including mentorship, opportunity to network, and workplace spaces. These organizations are frequently affiliated with educational establishments, research establishments, or private organizations. Joining an incubator or accelerator gives you access to a network of possible investors and partners, in addition to providing you with mentoring from seasoned professionals that is of immeasurable value.

3. **Networking:** Participating in networking events and communities can be of tremendous help to you on your journey. It is important to surround yourself with people who think and act similarly to you. Participate in industry-related networking events, seminars, and workshops to increase your chances of making connections with industry professionals, possible partners, and investors. Additionally, online networks and forums provide a venue for individuals involved in the entrepreneurial ecosystem to seek advice, share experiences, and learn from one another.

4. **Industry Associations and Organizations** Tailored to your Industry depending on the type of Business You Own. There May Be Associations and Organizations Tailored Specifically to Your Industry That Can Provide Specialized Support. For example, if you are launching a tech startup, associations such as NASSCOM can provide you with tools, mentorship, and insights into the sector. These associations can assist you in keeping abreast of the most recent tendencies, connecting with influential figures in your field, and gaining access to financing opportunities.

5. **Financial Assistance:** When it comes to providing financial assistance to new businesses, financial institutions such as banks, venture capitalists, and angel investors play

an essential role. Conduct research on, and make contact with, institutions that are in line with the business model or field in which you operate. To improve your chances of obtaining financial backing, it is important to be well-prepared with a comprehensive business plan, detailed financial predictions, and an engaging presentation.

Always keep in mind that the early phases of your company are not the only time you should be looking for help and tools. To build your business in a way that is both profitable and environmentally responsible, it is vital for you, as an entrepreneur, to keep your mind open, be flexible, and look for advice.

You can improve your chances of success, gain access to financial opportunities, and use the experience of other people if you take advantage of the many different support systems and resources that are available to you. Your ambitions of being an entrepreneur can become a reality with the correct amount of assistance and resources, despite the fact that beginning a business in India may present some difficulties.

Accepting and Enjoying One's Obstacles While Rejoicing in One's Achievements

Beginning the process of establishing a new company in India can be a thrilling and nerve-wracking experience for an ambitious business owner. The road to achievement is typically littered with a large number of obstacles, but it is essential to keep in mind that these roadblocks can be turned into steppingstones on the way to accomplishing your objectives. This subchapter will discuss the mental attitude that is necessary to accept obstacles and will offer some suggestions on how to enjoy your victories along the route.

Depending on the specific field you choose to operate in, you will need a specific set of abilities and background knowledge to launch a business in India. It does not matter if you want to start a firm in the manufacturing sector, the sustainable business sector, the consultancy industry, the social enterprise sector, or the technology sector; the problems you confront will be different. Successful business owners share a number of common traits, one of which is the capacity to accept and thrive in the face of adversity.

Positivity is the foundation for taking on difficult tasks and endeavors. It is essential to look at difficulties not as impediments but as possibilities for personal development. For instance, when launching a technology firm, you can run against technological roadblocks as well as intense rivalry. Consider each obstacle as a chance to learn something new and make yourself stand out from the crowd, rather than a reason to give up and become disheartened. In order to overcome these obstacles and obtain new perspectives, you should look for support from mentors, people who are already established in your sector, and networking events.

Recognizing and honouring one's achievements, no matter how modest, is of equal significance. Beginning a business in India is a journey that calls for tenacity and resolves on the part of the entrepreneur. The practice of commemorating significant achievements along the road serves to raise morale and maintain an entrepreneurial spirit. It might be anything as straightforward as recognizing the completion of a successful product prototype, the acquisition of your first customer, or even the securing of funding. You may cultivate a pleasant environment inside your team as well as a culture of success by publicly acknowledging and applauding the accomplishments of its members.

In addition, it is essential to gain knowledge from both one's achievements and one's failures. Whether an endeavour is fruitful or not, there are always important takeaways that can be incorporated into future plans. In the future, it will be beneficial for you to develop your tactics and make judgments based on accurate information if you reflect on what went well and what could have been done differently.

Keep in mind that launching a new company in India is not a step-by-step process. It is a sequence of victories and disappointments, but with the appropriate mindset, you can overcome challenges and fulfil your dreams of being an entrepreneur if you celebrate your successes and take pride in your accomplishments. Maintain your focus, develop your resilience, and never let fear stop you from meeting obstacles head-on.

Motivating Accounts of Businesspeople Who Have Achieved Success in India

India, a country that is well-known for its extensive cultural history and demographic variety, has also evolved as a hotbed for many forms of business endeavors. The country has seen a rise in the number of creative enterprises that are making their mark not only locally but also regionally and internationally.

These businesses range from new businesses that focus on sustainability to tech startups. In this subchapter, we will look into the motivational tales of successful businesspeople in India, exhibiting their journeys from the conception of an idea to the actualization of that idea.

1. **Rajan Anandan:** Is a significant person in the Indian Startup Ecosystem Rajan Anandan is a significant person in the Indian startup ecosystem. He was the former Managing Director of Google India. He has been an investor and mentor for a number of successful new businesses, some of which include Druva and Capillary Technologies. The motivational tale of Anandan demonstrates the significance of tenacity, creativity, and collaboration with strategic partners in the development of a prosperous technology firm.

2. **Swati Pandey** is the creator of Arboreal Agro Innovations, and she is currently bringing about a paradigm shift in the agriculture industry in India. Swati Pandey is a champion of sustainable business practices. Her company specializes in producing environmentally friendly farming solutions that cut down on the amount of water used and boost the

amount of produce harvested. The story of Pandey is illustrative of the possibility for environmentally conscious companies to make a good contribution to society as well as the natural world because of the strength of environmentally responsible practices.

3. **Ritu Verma** Is an Extraordinary Business Consultant Ritu Verma, co-founder of Ankur Capital and a pioneer in the fields of impact investing and consulting, is an extraordinary business consultant. Her company makes investments in early-stage entrepreneurs that are working to solve significant societal problems in areas such as agriculture, healthcare, and education. Verma's story demonstrates that it is possible to be successful in business while still being socially conscious, so demonstrating that consulting companies can be a driving force behind constructive social change.

4. **Ritesh Agarwal** Is a Manufacturing Magnate Ritesh Agarwal, the founder and CEO of OYO Rooms, began his journey as an entrepreneur at the youthful age of eighteen. Today, OYO is one of the leading hospitality brands in India, providing millions of travelers with accommodations at prices that are within their budgets. The narrative of Agarwal is illustrative of the importance of tenacity, adaptation, and creativity in the establishment of a prosperous manufacturing enterprise.

5. **Anshu Gupta** Is a Social Entrepreneur Who Has Revolutionized the Concept of donating and Recycling in India Anshu Gupta, the creator of Goonj, is a social entrepreneur who has transformed the idea of donating and recycling in India. His organization is dedicated to helping those who are less fortunate by salvaging unwanted garments and home goods and repurposing them into useful resources for those in need. The motivational tale of Gupta demonstrates how social companies have the capacity to have an enormous influence on society while simultaneously maintaining a financially sustainable model.

These enlightening accounts of successful businesspeople in India indicate that beginning a venture in India is not only possible, but it also has the potential to result in outstanding accomplishments. These tales can serve as a source of motivation and direction for anyone who are interested in beginning their own business ventures of any kind, including but not limited to social enterprises, sustainable businesses, consulting firms, manufacturing facilities, and IT startups. Keep in mind that in India's flourishing entrepreneurial scene, your idea may become a reality if you have the appropriate mindset, the perseverance to see it through, and the creativity to make it happen.

CHAPTER-9

GOVERNMENT SCHEMES AND SUPPORT IN INDIA

@dibyenduchoudhury

CHAPTER 9: GOVERNMENT SCHEMES AND SUPPORT IN INDIA

MSME stands for Micro, Small, and Medium Enterprises. It is a term introduced by the Government of India in agreement with the Micro, Small and Medium Enterprises Development (MSMED) Act of 2006. As per this act, MSMEs are the enterprises involved in the processing, production, and preservation of goods and commodities in the manufacturing or services sector[145].

The definition of MSMEs is based on the composite criteria of investment in plant and machinery or equipment and annual turnover. The revised classification applicable from 1st July 2020 is as follows:

Micro	Investment in Plant and Machinery or Equipment: Not more than Rs.1 crore and Annual Turnover ; not more than Rs. 5 crores
Small	Investment in Plant and Machinery or Equipment: Not more than Rs.10 crore and Annual Turnover ; not more than Rs. 50 crores
Medium	Investment in Plant and Machinery or Equipment: Not more than Rs.50 crore and Annual Turnover ; not more than Rs. 250 crores

The revised definition of MSME in 2022 is based on the composite criteria of investment in plant and machinery or equipment and annual turnover. The revised definition was officially updated by the center on May 13th, 2020, and came into effect from July 1st, 2020. The revised definition also includes retail and wholesale trade as MSMEs, as per the announcement made by the Ministry of MSME on July 2nd, 2021.

The revised definition of MSME in 2022 is as follows.

Micro	Investment in Plant and Machinery or Equipment: Not more than Rs.1 crore and Annual Turnover ; not more than Rs. 5 crores
Small	Investment in Plant and Machinery or Equipment: Not more than Rs.10 crore and Annual Turnover ; not more than Rs. 50 crores
Medium	Investment in Plant and Machinery or Equipment: Not more than Rs.50 crore and Annual Turnover ; not more than Rs. 250 crores

The revised definition of MSME in 2022 aims to provide better finance options, incentives, and support to the MSME sector, which contributes significantly to economic growth, employment generation, exports, and innovation in India. The revised definition also allows more enterprises to avail themselves of the benefits of various government schemes and policies for MSMEs.

MSMEs play a vital role in the economic development of India by contributing to employment generation, exports, innovation, and inclusive growth. They also face various challenges such as a lack of access to finance, technology, markets, infrastructure, and skilled workforce. The Government of India has launched various schemes and policies to support and promote MSMEs in India. Some of these schemes are:

- **MSME Loan Scheme:** This scheme provides working capital loans to MSMEs within 59 minutes of application.

- **Credit Guarantee Fund Scheme:** This scheme provides collateral-free loans to MSMEs through credit guarantee cover by CGTMSE.

- **MUDRA Loan Scheme:** This scheme provides micro loans to income-generating micro enterprises under PMMY.

- **Credit Link Capital Subsidy Scheme:** This scheme provides capital subsidy to MSMEs for technological upgradation of their plant and machinery.

- **National Small Industries Corporation Subsidy:** This subsidy provides raw material assistance and marketing support to MSMEs under NSIC.

These are some of the basic information about MSMEs in India. If you want to know more, you can visit the official website of the Ministry of MSME (https://msme.gov.in/) or contact your nearest nationalized bank or NBFC branch that offers these schemes. Thank you for using my service.

If you are searching for a loan to start up or develop your manufacturing or services business in India, you may be qualified for a variety of government initiatives that give financial support and incentives. These schemes may be found here. These programmes are intended to encourage micro, small, and medium companies (MSMEs), as well as innovative business practices, employment opportunities, and overall economic expansion.

For Indian Citizens, the following is a list of some of the best government programmes for which you can submit an application in 2022:

MSME Loan Scheme

Following an application, micro, small, and medium-sized enterprises (MSMEs) can receive a working capital loan from the Government of India in as little as 59 minutes.
- The value of the loan might range anywhere from one thousand rupees to one million rupees, based on the borrower's eligibility requirements and credit history.
- The annual interest rate is 8%, and there is a 3% discount reserved for business owners who identify as female.
- The time needed to process the loan ranges from 8 to 12 days, and the repayment term might be as long as 5 years.
- The loan can be put to use for everything the firm needs, including the purchase of equipment, raw materials, inventory,

marketing materials, and so on.

- New and existing enterprises that are registered on the Udyam portal are both eligible to apply for and receive the loan.

- The loan does not need any kind of collateral, and it also does not require a guarantor or any other kind of third-party security.

- The loan is distributed by a number of financial institutions, including banks and non-banking financial corporations (NBFCs), which are partners in the initiative.

- To submit an application for the loan, you will need to go to the scheme's official website (https://www.psbloansin59minutes.com/) and fill out an online application form with your personal information as well as information about your business. In addition to that, you will be required to provide papers such as your GST registration, income tax returns, bank statements, and any other pertinent documents. You will receive an acceptance in principle within 59 minutes, and then you will be able to choose the lender that you want to work with and finish the paperwork.

Credit Guarantee Fund Scheme

This programme offers loans to micro, small, and medium-sized enterprises (MSMEs) without requiring them to put up any collateral by utilizing the Credit Guarantee Fund Trust for Micro and Small Enterprises (CGTMSE).

- The value of the loan might range anywhere from ten thousand rupees to one million rupees, based on the borrower's eligibility requirements and credit history.

- The lender has discretion over the interest rate, although they are limited to a maximum spread of 4% over the base rate.

- The time it takes to process the loan might be as long as 30 days, and the repayment term can be as long as 7 years.

- The loan can be put to use for everything the firm needs, including the purchase of equipment, raw materials, inventory, marketing materials, and so on.

- New and existing enterprises that are registered on the Udyam portal are both eligible to apply for and receive the loan.

- The loan does not need any kind of collateral, and it also does not require a guarantor or any other kind of third-party security.

Despite this, the borrower is responsible for paying CGTMSE a one-time guaranteed charge equal to 1.5% of the loan amount as well as an annual service cost equal to 0.75 % of the amount still due.

- The loan is distributed by a number of financial institutions, including CGTMSE member banks and NBFCs.

- To submit an application for the loan, you will need to go to the branch of the bank or NBFC that is located closest to you and fill out the application form with your personal information as well as the information about your company. In addition to this, you need to supply documents such as your GST registration, income tax returns, bank statements, and any other pertinent paperwork. After determining that you are eligible for the loan and that you have good credit, the lender will grant you approval.

MUDRA Loan Scheme

Under the Pradhan Mantri Mudra Yojana (PMMY), this programme offers microloans to income-generating micro companies that are engaged in the manufacturing, processing, trading, or service sector.

- The value of the loan might range anywhere between Rs. 50,000 and Rs. Ten lakhs, depending on the stage the firm is in as well as its size.

- The lender has discretion over the interest rate; however, they are limited by a ceiling that equals MCLR plus 3% plus tenor premium.

- The time it takes to process the loan might be as long as 15 days, and the repayment term can be as long as 5 years.

- The loan can be put to use for everything the firm needs, including the purchase of equipment, raw materials, inventory, marketing materials, and so on.

- New and existing enterprises that are registered using the Udyam site or the Udyog Aadhaar Memorandum (UAM) are eligible to apply for and receive the loan.

- The loan does not need any kind of collateral, and it also does not require a guarantor or any other kind of third-party security. However, in order to secure the loan, the borrower is required to pay a processing fee to MUDRA Ltd., which is a subsidiary of the Small Industries Development Bank of India (SIDBI). This cost is equal to 0.5 percent of the total loan amount.

- The loan is distributed by a variety of financial organizations, including microfinance institutions (MFIs), commercial banks, non-bank financial companies (NBFCs), and other intermediaries that have cooperated with MUDRA Ltd.

To submit an application for the loan, you will need to go to the branch of the financial institution, NBFC, MFI, or intermediary that is located closest to you and fill out the application form with your personal as well as company information. In addition to this, you need to supply documents such as your GST registration, income tax returns, bank statements, and any other pertinent paperwork. After determining that you are eligible for the loan and that you have good credit, the lender will grant you approval.

Scheme for the Subsidization of Credit Link Capital

This programme offers a capital subsidy to micro, small, and medium-sized enterprises (MSMEs) so that they can improve the technological capabilities of their plant and machinery.

- The amount of the subsidy is equal to fifteen percent of the cost of the qualified plant and machinery, up to a maximum of fifteen million rupees per unit.

- The terms of the loan, including the interest rate, are negotiated between the borrower and the lender.

- The time it takes to process the loan might be as long as 30 days, and the repayment term can be as long as 10 years.

- The loan can be put towards the purchase of equipment and machinery, either brand new or secondhand, so long as it meets the requirements set forth by the scheme's Technical Subcommittee (TSC).

- New and established enterprises that are registered with the Udyam portal or UAM are eligible to apply for and receive the loan.

- The loan does not need any kind of collateral, and it also does not require a guarantor or any other kind of third-party security. The borrower, on the other hand, is required to pay a processing fee to the nodal agency of the scheme, which may be SIDBI or the National Bank for Agriculture and Rural Development (NABARD). This cost is equal to 0.5 percent of the loan amount.

- The loan is distributed through a number of financial institutions, including banks and NBFCs, that have established working relationships with the scheme's nodal agency.
- To submit an application for the loan, you will need to go to the branch of the bank or NBFC that is located closest to you and fill out the application form with your personal information as well as the information about your company. In addition to this, you need to supply documents such as your GST registration, income tax returns, bank statements, and any other pertinent paperwork. After determining that you are eligible for the loan and that you have good credit, the lender will grant you approval.

Subsidy provided by the National Small Industries Corporation

MSMEs can receive assistance with raw material costs and marketing support through this subsidy, which is administered by the National Small Industries Corporation (NSIC).

- The aid for raw materials includes both locally sourced and imported raw materials, as both are necessary for the manufacturing process. The subsidy amount is equal to fifteen percent of the total yearly purchase value of the raw materials, with a cap of one crore rupees (Rs.) per unit, per year.
- Participation in both domestic and international exhibitions, trade fairs, buyer-seller meets, and other similar events are all covered by the marketing support. The amount of the subsidy is 75% of the total cost of the venue rent as well as the transportation costs, up to a maximum of Rs. One lakh per unit for each event.
- The terms of the loan, including the interest rate, are negotiated between the borrower and the lender.
- The time it takes to process the loan might be as long as 30 days, and the payback duration can be as long as 12 months.
- In accordance with the parameters of the scheme, the loan may be put towards the acquisition of raw materials or the participation in marketing activities.

- New and established enterprises that are registered with the Udyam portal or UAM are eligible to apply for and receive the loan.

- The loan does not need any kind of collateral, and it also does not require a guarantor or any other kind of third-party security. On the other hand, the borrower is responsible for paying a processing charge to NSIC equal to one percent of the total loan amount.

- The loan is distributed through a variety of financial institutions, including banks and NBFCs, that are registered with NSIC.

- To submit an application for the loan, you will need to go to the NSIC branch that is closest to you or use the NSIC website (https://nsic.co.in/) to access the online portal and fill out the application form with your personal and company information. In addition to this, you need to supply documents such as your GST registration, income tax returns, bank statements, and any other pertinent paperwork. After confirming your eligibility and determining whether or not you have good credit, NSIC will give you, their approval.

You would need to complete these steps in order to apply for government initiatives in your capacity as an MSME:

- To begin, you will have to register your company as a micro, small, or medium-sized organization (MSME) through the Udyam portal (https://udyamregistration.gov.in/).

-You will receive a one-of-a-kind Udyam Registration Number (URN)/Udyog Aadhar Membership (UAM) and a certificate as a result of this process, both of which will allow you to take advantage of the numerous government programmes and policies geared at MSMEs.

- The second step is to locate the programme that fulfills the requirements of your company and is compatible with its needs. There are many different programmes that are run by the Ministry of Micro, Small, and Medium-Sized Enterprises (MoMSME) and its associated agencies. Some examples of these programmes include the Prime Minister Employment Generation Programme (PMEGP), the Credit Guarantee Fund Scheme (CGFS), the Micro and Small Enterprises Cluster Development Programme (MSE-

CDP), the International Cooperation Scheme (IC), and many more.

- The third step is to go to the program's official website or online portal and fill out the online application form with all of your personal and company information. If you wish to apply for the programme, you should do this. -In addition, in order to comply with the requirements of the programme, you are required to either upload or send in your Udyam registration certificate, as well as your GST registration, income tax returns, bank statements, and project report.

-You are required, as the fourth step, to wait for approval from the relevant body or agency that is in charge of carrying out the scheme. The length of time required for the approval procedure is typically up to thirty days, but this could change depending on the plan. You can check the status of your application by checking either your email or sending an SMS message.

-Fifth, once your application has been reviewed and accepted, the loan or subsidy amount will be sent into your bank account in accordance with the terms and conditions of the scheme. According to the terms of the agreement, you will be responsible for complying with the reporting and monitoring obligations of the scheme.

These are some of the general actions that need to be taken in order for an MSME to apply for government initiatives. Nevertheless, depending on the approach that you go with, you can be required to carry out a number of certain stages or procedures. As a result, it is highly recommended to study the scheme instructions in detail and contact the scheme nodal person or the helpline number if you have any questions or need any clarifications.

I am grateful that you chose my book to learn.

Other Book of the Author

Dr. Dibyendu Choudhury, one of India's eminent Management Gurus and mythologists, offers an interesting look at the top 25 personalities modern organizations may need in their leadership positions post pandemic. He draws on stories from the Mahabharata and the Ramayana. Businesses often need visionary leaders with an entrepreneurial spirit to steer them through challenging times. In the wake of the pandemic, most businesses don't know how to pick a leader who can successfully communicate, inspire workers, and strike the correct balance between strictness and compassion. This applies to any workplace i.e., Micro to Medium Enterprises and even large corporates. This is applied to any workplace. Dibyendu demonstrates the timeless management lessons that may be gleaned from stories written thousands of years ago. Be the Leader, Not the Boss! 25 Secrets to Being an Entrepreneurial Leader with Insights from Mythology draws on mythological figures and contemporary stories to reveal timeless truths about what it takes to be an effective and innovative leader. All his books available in Amazon India Site.

WEB REFERENCES:

14 Lessons From Entrepreneurs On Starting Your Own Business; https://www.weforum.org/agenda/2021/09/14-lessons-from-entrepreneurs-on-starting-your-own-business-0c80163aed/

4 Ways a Business Can Create a Positive Social Impact; https://www.linkedin.com/pulse/4-ways-business-can-create-positive-social-impact-aitzaz-ahmed/

5 Features Of A Great Mentoring Programme; https://mentorloop.com/blog/5-features-great-mentoring-program/

5 Government Loan Schemes For MSMEs & Startups In India. https://www.msmex.in/learn/govt-loan-schemes-for-msmes-startups/.

A Complete Guide On "How To Start A Consulting Business In India?";https://ebizfiling.com/blog/consulting-business-in-india/

A Step-By-Step Guide of The Documents Required for Company Registration Process In India; https://digest.myhq.in/company-registration-process-in-india/

All You Need To Know About Legal Environment; https://blog.ipleaders.in/all-you-need-to-know-about-legal-environment/

An Actionable 10-Step Guide to Launch a Tech Startup; https://www.neoito.com/blog/launching-tech-startup-complete-guide/

Business Environment in Present India; https://www.linkedin.com/pulse/business-environment-present-india-bedaant-srivastav/

Companies Act 2013 - Indian Companies Act Definition, Companies Act 1956; https://byjus.com/free-ias-prep/indian-companies-act/

Company Law in India; https://ssrana.in/corporate-laws/company-laws-india/company-law-india/

Doing Business in India: Advantages & Disadvantages; https://www.wolterskluwer.com/en/expert-insights/doing-business-in-india

Doing Business in India: Advantages and Disadvantages; https://www.niir.org/blog/doing-business-india-advantages-disadvantages/

Four Steps to Sustainable Business Model Innovation; https://www.bcg.com/publications/2021/four-strategies-for-sustainable-business-model-innovation

How Narrowing Your Focus Can Lead To More Growth; https://www.forbes.com/sites/forbesagencycouncil/2021/09/08/how-narrowing-your-focus-can-lead-to-more-growth/?sh=3c01510d65a3

How The Indian Talent Pool is Enriching the Global Economy; https://www.ibef.org/blogs/how-the-indian-talent-pool-is-enriching-the-global-economy

How to Break Down Your Goals Into Actionable Steps;https://facilethings.medium.com/how-to-break-down-your-goals-into-actionable-steps

How to Position Yourself as the Expert in Your Industry; https://www.leadersinstitute.com/become-the-go-to-expert-in-your-industry/

How to Reduce Your Carbon Footprint at Home; https://www.linkedin.com/pulse/how-reduce-your-carbon-footprint-home-union-solar-renewables/

How to register your business in India; https://startuptalky.com/register-business-india/

How To Talk to Potential Investors: 5 Tips; https://online.hbs.edu/blog/post/talking-to-potential-investors

Identifying Your Business Idea: The First Step to Entrepreneurial Success; https://www.linkedin.com/pulse/identifying-your-business-idea-first-step-success-shrikant-pandey/

India's Legal and Regulatory Framework; https://www.ukibc.com/india-guide/how-india/legal/

Innovation, Agility and Adaptability; https://www.linkedin.com/pulse/innovation-agility-adaptability-balkrishan-goenka/

Key Strategies for Growth and Sustainability as an Entrepreneur; https://www.linkedin.com/pulse/key-strategies-growth-sustainability-entrepreneur-knowlton-phd/

Legal Requirements for Starting a Business in India; https://www.lexology.com/library/detail.aspx?g=5aef1aea-0e13-483c-979a-7785d0576b0f

Leveraging Partnerships: A Survival Strategy for Startups in Volatile Times; https://www.linkedin.com/pulse/leveraging-partnerships-survival-strategy-startups-volatile-bharani/

Major Laws and Regulations Governing Conduct of Business in India; https://www.yourarticlelibrary.com/law/major-laws-and-regulations-governing-conduct-of-business-in-india/22823

Market Research and Consumer Behavior;https://www.linkedin.com/pulse/market-research-consumer-behavior-karthik-p/

Ministry of Micro, Small & Medium Enterprises. https://www.msme.gov.in/.

MSME Definition Revised: What is New MSME; Know Difference between Old .... https://www.jagranjosh.com/current-affairs/new-definition-of-msme-difference-between-old-new-msme-increased-investment-1589378468-1.

MSME Definition: MSME Full-form and Meaning 2023 - Razorpay. https://razorpay.com/learn/new-msme-definition-turnover-2020/.

MSME Definition: MSME Full-form and Meaning 2023 - Razorpay. https://razorpay.com/learn/new-msme-definition-turnover-2020/.

MSME New Definition – New Definition of MSME 2023 - Setindiabiz. https://www.setindiabiz.com/learning/new-definition-of-msme.

Online Application - Ministry of Micro, Small & Medium Enterprises. https://msme.gov.in/online-application.

Overcoming Challenges to Implementing Mentoring Programs in Private and Public Sectors; http://mentoring.coleygts.com/mentoring/challenges-mentoring-public-private-sectors/

Overview of Process for Establishing a Manufacturing Unit in India; https://taxguru.in/corporate-law/overview-process-establishing-manufacturing-unit-india.html

PM participates in 'Udyami Bharat' programme; https://pib.gov.in/PressReleasePage.aspx?PRID=1838174

Pradhan Mantri Mudra Yojana - myScheme. https://www.myscheme.gov.in/schemes/pmmy.

Principles; https://sustainabledevelopment.un.org/content/documents/5839GSDR%202015_SD_concept_definiton_rev.pdf

Private Sector Can Play a Significant Role In Addressing The Nutritional Woes Of India. Analyse; https://www.insightsonindia.com/2018/06/18/4-private-sector-can-play-a-significant-role-in-addressing-the-nutritional-woes-of-india-analyse-250-words/

Retail & Business: India Retail and E-Commerce Trends 2022; https://www.indianretailer.com/article/whats-hot/retail-trends/india-retail-and-e-commerce-trends-2022.a8176

Revised Definition of MSME – Addition of Retail and Wholesale Trade. https://www.indiafilings.com/learn/revised-definition-of-msme-addition-of-retail-

and-wholesale-trade/.

Scale Up Your Business – With Top Startup Consulting Services; https://blog.tech2globe.com/scale-up-your-business-with-top-startup-consulting-services/

Schemes for MSMEs in India - Invest India. https://www.investindia.gov.in/schemes-msmes-india.

Schemes for MSMEs in India are the source of this information. https://www.investindia.gov.in/schemes-msmes-india.

Sustainability must be core of India Inc's business strategy; https://energy.economictimes.indiatimes.com/news/renewable/sustainability-must-be-core-of-india-incs-business-strategy/99206890

The Business Of Sustainability; https://www.mckinsey.com/capabilities/sustainability/our-insights/the-business-of-sustainability-mckinsey-global-survey-results

The Concept of Sustainable Development: Definition and Defining

The Growth Of Startup Ecosystem In India; https://startuptalky.com/the-growth-of-indian-startup-ecosystem/

The Legal and Regulatory Framework For Environmental Protection In India; http://www.moef.gov.in/wp-content/uploads/wssd/doc2/ch2.html

The Power of Consumers: Making a Difference through Fair Trade and Socially Responsible Lifestyle Choices; https://timesofindia.indiatimes.com/readersblog/theintersection/the-power-of-consumers-making-a-difference-through-fair-trade-and-socially-responsible-lifestyle-choices-55044/

The Role Of Communication Transparency And Organizational Trust In Publics' Perceptions, Attitudes And Social Distancing Behaviour: A Case Study Of The COVID-19 Outbreak; https://www.ncbi.nlm.nih.gov/pmc/articles/PMC8012987/

The Top Five Government Loan Programmes Available To Businesses In India In 2022. https://www.indiatoday.in/information/story/top-5-government-business-loan-schemes-in-india-in-2022-1897500-2022-01-08.

The Ultimate Guide To Scaling A Startup In India: Success Stories And Expert Tips; https://www.theceo.in/blogs/the-ultimate-guide-to-scaling-a-startup-in-india-success-stories-and-expert-tips

The World Bank in India; https://www.worldbank.org/en/country/india/overview

Top 10 Inspiring Indian Entrepreneurs Success Stories: That Will Inspire you;https://digitalscholar.in/indian-entrepreneurs-success-stories/

Top 20 Best Venture Capital & Private Equity Companies In India 2023; https://www.inventiva.co.in/trends/venture-capital-private-equity-company/

Understanding the Legal and Regulatory Requirements for Starting a Manufacturing Business in India; https://www.eiriindia.org/blog/understanding-legal-regulatory-requirements-starting-manufacturing-business-india

Way ahead for strengthening India's Cyber Security Framework & Regulations; https://www.linkedin.com/pulse/way-ahead-strengthening-indias-cyber-security-framework-deepak-sai/

What Are Crowdfunding Platforms?; https://www.financestrategists.com/financial-advisor/startup-funding-strategies/crowdfunding-platforms/

What is MSME/SME Full Form, Meaning, Role and Importance in India. https://www.paisabazaar.com/business-loan/what-is-msme/.

What is MSME? Meaning, Full Form, Features, Role & Importance in India. https://www.lendingkart.com/msme-loan/what-is-msme/.

What is the definition of MSME. https://msme.gov.in/faqs/q1-what-definition-msme.

What is the definition of MSME. https://msme.gov.in/faqs/q1-what-definition-msme.

What is the difference between a startup accelerator and an incubator; https://fastercapital.com/content/What-is-the-difference-between-a-startup-accelerator-and-an-incubator.html

What's MSME | Ministry of Micro, Small & Medium Enterprises. https://msme.gov.in/know-about-msme.

Which criteria matter when impact investors screen social enterprises?; https://www.sciencedirect.com/science/article/pii/S0929119920302571

Work-Life Balance or Better Pay? Which factor should your business focus on?; https://www.linkedin.com/pulse/work-life-balance-better-pay-which-factor-should-your/